Victorious and Vulnerable

HOOVER STUDIES IN POLITICS, ECONOMICS, AND SOCIETY

General Editors
Peter Berkowitz and Tod Lindberg

Victorious and Vulnerable

Why Democracy Won in the
20th Century and How It Is Still Imperiled

Azar Gat

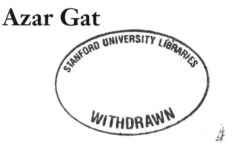

HOOVER STUDIES
IN POLITICS, ECONOMICS,
AND SOCIETY

Published in cooperation with
HOOVER INSTITUTION
Stanford University • Stanford, California

ROWMAN & LITTLEFIELD PUBLISHERS, INC.
Lanham • Boulder • New York • Toronto • Plymouth, UK

ROWMAN & LITTLEFIELD PUBLISHERS, INC.

THE HOOVER INSTITUTION ON WAR, REVOLUTION AND PEACE, founded at Stanford University in 1919 by Herbert Hoover, who went on to become the thirty-first president of the United States, is an interdisciplinary research center for advanced study on domestic and international affairs. The views expressed in its publications are entirely those of the authors and do not necessarily reflect the views of the staff, officers, or Board of Overseers of the Hoover Institution.

www.hoover.org

Published in the United States of America by Rowman & Littlefield Publishers, Inc.
A wholly owned subsidiary of The Rowman & Littlefield Publishing Group, Inc.
4501 Forbes Boulevard, Suite 200, Lanham, Maryland 20706
www.rowmanlittlefield.com
Estover Road
Plymouth PL6 7PY
United Kingdom
Distributed by National Book Network

Copyright © 2010 by the Board of Trustees of the Leland Stanford Junior University

Published in cooperation with the Hoover Institution at Stanford University.

First printing, 2010
16 15 14 13 12 11 10 09   9 8 7 6 5 4 3 2 1
Manufactured in the United States of America

British Library Cataloguing in Publication Information Available

Library of Congress Cataloging-in-Publication Data Available

ISBN: 978-1-4422-0114-9 (cloth : alk. paper)
ISBN: 978-1-4422-0116-3 (electronic)

♾ The paper used in this publication meets the minimum requirements of American National Standard for Information Sciences—Permanence of Paper for Printed Library Materials, ANSI/NISO Z39.48-1992.

To my parents, Josepha and Eli

Contents

Preface

Since the end of the Cold War, capitalist liberal democracy has enjoyed pre-eminence if not hegemony in the global system, and this has conferred a sense of inevitability on its success. By the close of the twentieth century, the world's communist regimes were withering away and dissolving themselves. Formerly communist countries embraced capitalism, and some even embraced democracy. Liberal democracy no longer seemed to face any socio-political or ideological challengers, having already crushed its authoritarian and fascist rivals in the two World Wars (with the help of Russia/the Soviet Union). Indeed, all the world's wealthy and powerful countries were liberal democratic. With such a sweeping record and decisive historical outcome, democracy's victory seemed not only secure but also inevitable, the product of its superior compatibility with modernity and capitalism, if not its moral superiority. This was the mood most famously captured by Francis Fukuyama's End of History thesis.

Yet it took but the blink of an eye in historical terms for liberal democracy's moment of triumph to be darkened by new threats, challenges, and doubts. With the advent of the twenty-first century, history is rumored to have returned. The Islamic backlash, bursting to the forefront with the September 11 attacks, can be viewed as the death throes of a retreating, deeply dysfunctional premodern order. The threat arises from some of the world's weakest societies and presents no viable alternative model of modernity. Only the prospect of unconventional terror makes the threat serious. The return of capitalist nondemocratic great powers—above all the gigantic and quickly modernizing China, but also Russia—poses a challenge of an entirely different scale. Is this development, too, merely a phase in the process of modernization that will ultimately lead these countries to democratize? In an article in Foreign Affairs (Summer 2007), I suggested that this was not necessarily the case, and that liberal democracy's victory in the twentieth century was more tenuous than it is assumed to be. Since then, the return of authoritarian great powers has become a much-discussed theme.

In the article, I mentioned very abstractly the possibility of a crisis in the global economic system that may undermine confidence in the democracies and raise the stock of anti-democratic statism and economic protectionism worldwide. In the meantime, the world economy has been experiencing massive shock waves from the American housing and credit crisis that began to unravel in the autumn of 2007. It is impossible to predict the outcome of the crisis, which experts assess to be the most severe since the Wall Street crash of 1929. My own guess is that the economic and political consequences will be nowhere as far-reaching. And yet the formerly prevailing spirit of high optimism has been all but dissipated in this sphere as well.

Another theme concerning the future of world democracy that has attracted great attention and shaped foreign policy in recent decades is that of democratic peace: the notion that advanced and economically developed liberal democracies hardly ever fight each other. If true, democracies are crucially different from nondemocratic countries in their foreign policy and conflict behavior. This idea was long regarded with skepticism by scholars and is wholly denied by one of the principal schools in the discipline of international relations: "realism." But the evidence for it has become overwhelming. Indeed, it has begun dawning on scholars that the democratic peace phenomenon is merely one conspicuous element within a larger whole. And it is some major and variously unrecognized aspects of the democracies' distinctive conflict behavior that this book sets out to explore. If democracy's victory is more contingent and tenuous than previously believed, and if democracies still face serious security challenges, then a deeper understanding of their peculiar strengths and vulnerabilities becomes not only intellectually interesting but also politically and strategically crucial.

This book brings together and builds upon my earlier writings on democracies' war and conflict behavior. Earlier versions appeared in my *War in Human Civilization*, published by Oxford University Press, *Foreign Affairs* (chapters 1 and 4), *World Politics* (chapter 5), and the *Times Literary Supplement* (chapter 8).

It is my pleasant duty to thank people and organizations that assisted along the way. My friend Peter Berkowitz of the Hoover Institution suggested I write this book. Editors Rachel Abrams, Katherine Goldgeier, Tod Lindberg, and Peter read the manuscript and made invaluable suggestions. A research period at Hoover helped to bring the book about. The Glasshouse Forum in Stockholm has taken an interest in the return of capitalist nondemocratic great powers and has organized several international meetings to discuss it. At Tel Aviv University, I received support from the Ezer Weitzman Chair of National Security, of which I am the incumbent, and my friends and colleagues. My friend Alexander (Alex) Yakobson of the Hebrew University in Jerusalem read various draft chapters and made excellent comments, as always. The book was completed in Munich, during a research stay made possible by the Alexander von Humboldt Foundation and hosted by Professor Christopher Daase of the Ludwig Maximilian University. I thank them all.

1
Why Democracy Won
in the Twentieth Century

The liberal democratic camp emerged victorious from all three of the gigantic power struggles of the twentieth century—the two World Wars and the Cold War—defeating autocracy, fascism, and communism alike. What accounts for this decisive outcome?

It is tempting to look for the roots of this triumph in the special traits of liberal democracy. In the nineteenth century, the 1950s and 1960s, and the post-Cold War era, it was widely believed that liberalism and democracy were inextricably intertwined with the process of modernization. According to this view, most recently elaborated by Francis Fukuyama and Michael Mandelbaum, industrialization, urbanization, the rise of the middle class, the spread of education, and ever-greater affluence fostered, and in turn depended upon, a free and self-governing society.[1] There was, in effect, only one sustainable route to modernity. Those countries unfortunate enough to have developed along paths different from the one originally taken by Britain and the United States eventually had to converge onto the liberal path, either because they proved weaker than the democracies, or because they were bound to experience intractable internal contradictions that ultimately caused them to implode or to undergo dramatic transformation. Liberal democracy has been presumed to possess intrinsic advantages that confer an air of historical inevitability and give much cause for optimism. Indeed, if "world history is the world's court," as Hegel put it, then history's verdict appears clear-cut. But is it really? In fact, democracy's twentieth century victory has obscured the reasons why it won.

Why the Authoritarian/Totalitarian Challengers Lost

We begin with the audit of great power conflict and war that was central to twentieth century history. Did the liberal democracies survive all rivals because they more than compensated for their inferior ability to repress foreign peoples and nations with a greater ability to elicit cooperation through the bonds and discipline of the global market system? The answer is probably yes with respect to the Cold War but not to the world-wars period, when the system turned protectionist. Did liberal democracies succeed because ultimately they always stuck together? During the Cold War, the answer may again have been yes. The democratic-capitalist camp was in any case greatly superior, and profited from the growing antagonism within the communist bloc between the Soviet Union and China. During World War I, however, the ideological divide between the protagonists was much weaker than it would later become. The Anglo-French alliance was far from preordained, being above all a function of the balance of power rather than the fruit of liberal cooperation. Only slightly earlier, power politics had brought these bitterly antagonistic countries to the brink of war and prompted Britain to seek an alliance with Germany. Liberal Italy left the Triple Alliance and joined the Entente despite its rivalry with France and as a result of the Anglo-French alliance: Italy's peninsular location made conflict with the leading maritime power, Britain, highly undesirable. During World War II, France was quickly defeated, whereas the right-wing totalitarian powers fought on the same side. Dedicated studies of democracies' alliance behavior tally with these observations.[2]

Nor did the democracies hold a moral high ground that inspired greater exertion from their people, as some scholars have claimed.[3] During the 1930s and early 1940s, fascism and communism were the exciting new ideologies that generated massive popular enthusiasm, whereas democracy stood on the ideological defensive, appearing old, outdated, and dispirited. If anything, fascist regimes proved more inspiring than their democratic adversaries in war, and their militaries' battlefield performance is widely judged to have been superior. France quickly collapsed in 1940, but Germany and Japan fought desperately to the last (with the Soviet Union fighting as desperately).

Did the liberal democracies ultimately prove more effective in economic mobilization, despite their strong initial reluctance to engage in war and their lower levels of peacetime mobilization? In fact, all the belligerents proved highly effective in mobilizing their societies and economies for total war. Conservative and semi-autocratic Germany during World War I committed its resources as intensively as its liberal-parliamentary rivals. After its victories during the initial stage of World War II, Nazi Germany's economic mobilization proved lax and poorly coordinated during the critical years 1940-1942. Although Germany was well-positioned at the time to fundamentally alter the global balance of power by destroying the Soviet Union and striding across all of continental Europe, it failed because its armed forces were meagerly supplied by war production for a task that proved far more demanding than expected.[4] The reasons for this fateful failure were complex, but they were at least partly a result of structural problems stemming from competing authorities inherent in Germany's totalitarian regime: Hitler's "divide and rule" tactics and Nazi party functionaries' jealous guarding of their assigned domains had a chaotic effect. Furthermore, from the fall of France in June 1940 to the German setback before Moscow in December 1941, there was a widespread feeling in Germany that the war had practically been won. All the same, from 1942 on, when it was too late, Germany's highly intensified economic mobilization levels caught up with and surpassed those of the liberal democracies in terms of the share of gross national product (GNP) devoted to the war (though production volume remained much lower because of the huge size of the U.S. economy). Similarly, thanks to ruthless methods, Imperial Japan and Soviet Russia increased their levels of mobilization during World War II beyond those of the liberal democracies. As historian Niall Ferguson recently concluded, the totalitarian regimes demonstrated greater ability than the liberal democracies to mobilize for war, which gave them a considerable military advantage.[5]

So why did the democracies win the great struggles of the twentieth century? There is a notable difference between their communist and capitalist adversaries. The defeat of communism had to do with deep structural factors. The Soviet system, which had successfully generated the early and intermediate stages of industrialization (albeit at a horrendous cost in human life and misery) and excelled at the regimentalized techniques of mass production during World War II, kept apace with its capitalist protagonists militarily during the Cold War. But because of the system's rigidity and lack of incentives, it proved ill-equipped to cope with the information age's diversified economy and more advanced stages of development. The capitalist camp—which expanded after 1945 to include most of the developed world—possessed much greater economic power than the communist bloc, and the inherent inefficiency of the communist economies prevented them from fully exploiting their vast resources and catching up. Together the Soviet Union and China were larger and therefore had the potential to be more powerful than the democratic-capitalist camp. Furthermore, had they succeeded economically, other countries would surely have followed. Ultimately, however, the communist bloc practically dismantled itself. Independently from each other, both communist China and the Soviet

Union found their systems inefficient, almost irrespective of their militarized conflict with the capitalist-democratic world. China, for example, could not but be impressed by the staggering performance of Chinese-populated Taiwan, Hong Kong, and Singapore, to say nothing of the stark difference in economic development between neighboring North and South Korea.

By contrast, had capitalist nondemocratic Germany and Japan triumphed in the World Wars, it is unlikely they would have proved as thoroughly inefficient as the communist great powers. For this reason, the capitalist nondemocratic great powers (again, particularly Germany) can now be judged to have a been more viable challenge to the liberal democracies than was the Soviet Union. Indeed, Nazi Germany was so judged by the Western powers before and during World War II. The liberal democracies did not possess an inherent advantage over Germany in terms of economic and technological development, as they did in relation to their other great power rivals.

So why did the capitalist nondemocratic powers—Germany and Japan—lose? The literature that celebrates the triumph of capitalist liberal democracy as the ultimate vindication of democracy's intrinsic superiority under modern conditions offers very little analysis of that historical outcome, and tacitly assumes it to be akin to the collapse of communism for very different reasons.[6] In the final analysis, however, the capitalist nondemocratic powers lost in war because they were medium-size countries with limited resources battling a far superior but hardly preordained economic-military coalition: the democratic powers and Russia in World War I and the democratic powers and the Soviet Union, which took the brunt of the fighting, during World War II. Whereas the communist powers failed because their economic system limited them, the capitalist authoritarian/totalitarian powers, Germany and Japan, were defeated because they were too small. Contingency played a decisive role in tipping the balance against them and in favor of the democracies.

The most obvious and decisive of these contingent factors was the United States. After all, it was little more than a chance of history that this scion of English liberalism would sprout on the other side of the Atlantic, institutionalize its liberal heritage with independence, and then expand across the most habitable territories of the Americas, thinly populated by tribal natives, while drawing in massive immigration from Europe. It was but a chance of history that the world's largest concentration of economic-military power was thus created on a continental scale. Obviously, the United States' liberal regime and other structural traits made it attractive to immigrants and thus had a lot to do with its economic success (consider Latin America) and even with its size; yet if the United States had not been located in a particularly fortunate and vast geographical-ecological niche, it would scarcely have achieved its great magnitude in population or territory, as Canada, Australia, and New Zealand demonstrate. And although location was crucial, it was not everything but only one necessary condition among many that created a giant and, indeed, *United* States as the paramount political factor of the twentieth century.

Thus, contingent circumstances were at least as responsible as liberalism for the United States' emergence in the New World and for its later ability to "rescue the Old World," as Winston Churchill put it. Throughout the twentieth century, the United States' power consistently surpassed that of the next two strongest states combined, and this decisively tilted the global balance of power in favor of whichever side Washington was on. The liberal democracies possessed greater aggregate resources than their rivals because of that crucial fact no less than because of their advanced economies (which, again, were not more advanced than Germany's).

The "United States factor" is widely overlooked in scholarly studies of democracy's victory during the twentieth century.[7] These studies reflect a professional predisposition to think in theoretical terms, and they overlook the possibility that contingent historical causes were largely responsible for the outcome. The victory of liberal democracy was anything but pre-ordained in either 1914 or 1939, though it may have been more secure in 1945; yet if any factor gave the liberal democracies their edge, it was above all the actual circumstances of the United States rather than any inherent advantage of liberal democracy. Put differently, if it were not for the existence of the United States, the liberal democracies would most likely have lost the great struggles of the twentieth century. Without the United States, Britain and France would probably have lost to Germany in either of the two World Wars. This is a sobering thought, making the world created by the twentieth century's conflicts appear much more contingent—and tenuous—than unilineal theories of development and the Whig view of history as Progress would have us believe. We might have had a very different and non-democratic twentieth century, a very different world today, and a very different story to tell by way of grand theories of development. It is a well-known yet often-forgotten truism that history is written by the victors. If it were not for the "U.S. factor," the judgment of later generations on liberal democracy would probably have echoed the negative verdict on democracy's performance issued by the Greeks in the fourth century BC, in the wake of Sparta's defeat of Athens in the Peloponnesian War. The constructed grand narrative of the twentieth century would have underlined the liberal democracies' political divisiveness and decadence, and the superiority of authoritarian/totalitarian cohesiveness, rather than the triumph of freedom. We are inclined to rationalize backwards, but the lessons of history are a tricky thing.

Skeptics might doubt that the course of history is really so affected by contingency, and claim—with Hegel—that accidents are not that accidental but rather happen to those who are accident-prone. For example, they cite Nazi Germany's critical production failure in 1940-1942 as an indication of a deep-seated structural problem in its totalitarian system that ultimately cost it World War II.[8] Maybe, but one should guard against lopsided interpretations. Germany remedied its production failure from 1942 on; in World War I it had experienced no similar failure, nor did Japan in World War II; in both wars the capitalist nondemocratic great powers performed great feats and won overwhelming victories. On the other side, the democracies went from blunder to blunder in both World Wars: their publics and governments were dangerously late to rise to the challenge and their armed forces were ill-prepared, particularly during the 1930s; their initial defeats were potentially catastrophic; and their conduct was anything but free from serious errors thereafter.

Thus all sides committed serious mistakes and occasionally blundered, sometimes for reasons relating to their respective systems. Contrary to the comforting notion that the democratic system eventually proved superior, the main difference lay in the fact that Germany's mistakes were simply unforgiving, given its relative size and the odds it was facing. As Germany was smaller than its adversaries, its performance was less failure-tolerant. To break out of its limited territorial confines and fatally cripple the superior coalition assembled against it in either of the World Wars, Germany critically required a consecutive string of major successes. Indeed, it came remarkably close to achieving that goal in both World Wars, with particularly horrifying potential consequences had it won World War II, but also with major consequences for the future of liberalism and democracy worldwide had it won World War I. By contrast, the colossal power of the U.S. made it possible for the democracies to sustain catastrophic failures—including the fall of their Russian ally in World War I and the fall of France and the shattering of the U.S. Pacific fleet at Pearl Harbor in World War II—and still come back.

Is Democratization Inevitable?

The central idea of the literature on the triumph of democracy is that democracy and capitalism are intrinsically and intimately connected in a way that eventually makes the one impossible without the other. However, our preliminary analysis of the past suggests that the relationship between the two may be looser. Capitalism has indeed proved to be an unbeatable engine for creating wealth and power. It has expanded relentlessly since early modernity, its lower-priced goods and the superior economic power eroding and transforming all other socioeconomic regimes—a process most memorably described by Karl Marx in the *Communist Manifesto*.* Contrary to Marx's expectations, capitalism had the same effect on communism, eventually "burying" it without a shot being fired. On the other hand, the evidence regarding democracy's advantage has been more ambivalent, particularly in comparison to nondemocratic capitalism.

Of course, the audit of war is not the only one that societies undergo. One can ask how the capitalist authoritarian and totalitarian powers would have developed had they not been defeated in the World Wars. With more time and further development, would they not have shed their former identities, as the communist regimes eventually did, and perhaps even embraced liberal democracy? The issue is the feasibility of economically developed, capitalist nondemocratic countries; there is nothing special in the existence of poorer nondemocratic countries.

Was capitalist-industrial Imperial Germany before World War I ultimately moving towards increasing parliamentary control by the Reichstag and eventual democratization? Or would it have developed

* The economic crisis that erupted in 2007-2008 has generated renewed predictions of the demise of capitalism, which in my view are unwarranted. It is necessary to point out that throughout the book capitalism is meant in the broadest, pluralist sense, incorporating the primacy of private property and private enterprise, the market, and extensive commercialism. Within this broad frame, capitalism has had various local and historical variants.

in the opposite direction into an authoritarian-oligarchic regime, dominated by an alliance between the officialdom, the armed forces, and industry—as Imperial Japan did during the 1930s, despite its liberal interlude in the 1920s? Eventual liberalization seems even more doubtful in the case of Nazi Germany, had it survived, let alone triumphed. There is little cause to believe these brutal regimes (obviously Nazi Germany was far more so than Japan) would have collapsed because of their brutality, even if some future mellowing was possible. Michael Mandelbaum claims that fascism totally discredited itself by bringing only death, destruction, and horror. This, however, is the judgment after fascism lost. Its victory might well have been celebrated as a striking vindication of deep-seated, antiliberal traditions that were particularly strong and vibrant in Germany and Japan. Moreover, the imperial orders and *Herrenvolk* status that these countries intended to establish in Europe and East Asia, respectively, would have rested on that ideological foundation, giving it added resilience.

As war cut short these major historical experiments, making their potential alternate trajectories a matter of speculation, scholars turn to the peacetime record of other authoritarian-capitalist regimes that survived in the post-1945 period. Studies covering this period show that democracies generally outperform other systems economically, but that capitalist authoritarian regimes are at least as successful—if not more so—in generating development, for the above-cited reasons.[9] Especially in East Asia, the capitalist authoritarian regimes have prospered, outperforming democracies. All the same, it is generally agreed that capitalist authoritarian regimes tend to democratize after crossing a certain threshold of economic and social development. This seems to have been a recurring pattern: in East Asia, southern Europe, and Latin America.

However, the attempt to deduce a general pattern of development from these findings may be misleading, because the sample set may be skewed. Since 1945, the enormous gravitational pull exerted by the United States and the liberal hegemony has bent patterns of development worldwide. Crushed in war and threatened by Soviet hegemony, the capitalist authoritarian/totalitarian great powers, Germany and Japan, were impelled by the United States to undertake a sweeping restructuring and democratization. Consequently, those smaller countries that chose capitalism over communism were left with no rival model to emulate or international powers to join other than the liberal. Their democratization after a certain level of economic development was probably as much a result of the overwhelming influence of the Western-liberal hegemony as of internal processes. As of 2009, Singapore was the only example of a truly developed economy that still maintained a semi-authoritarian regime. Singapore is a small-scale polity, and it too is likely to change under the influence of a hegemonic liberal order. But are Singapore-like great powers that prove resistant to the influence of this order possible?

During the nineteenth century, liberal Britain represented the universal model for the future. But as its economic dominance waned, the right- and left-wing nondemocratic great powers offered powerful alternative models. The number and relative share of democracies in the international system again increased in the wake of World War II, but then decreased under the impact of the communist challenge, de-colonization, and problems of development in the Third World.[10] A third wave of democratization began in the 1970s, gathering momentum with the Soviet collapse. More than half of all states (and the majority the world's population) now have elective government, and close to half have sufficient liberal rights to justify their designation as fully free. Has the dominance of the liberal model gained such a wide-reaching hold that a threshold has been crossed and a similar relapse is unlikely? For some time a reverse wave has been anticipated, and it may already be taking place.

The most significant development is the emergence of new nondemocratic giants, above all the formerly-communist and fast-industrializing, authoritarian-capitalist China, whose massive growth represents the greatest change in the global balance of power. Russia, too, is retreating from its post-communist liberalism and assuming an increasingly authoritarian character. Will these countries ultimately converge into the liberal democratic range through a combination of internal development, increasing affluence, and outside influence? Or are they big enough to chart a different course and challenge the hegemonic model, creating a new, nondemocratic but economically advanced and militarily powerful Second World? Might they, for example, recreate in some form a authoritarian-capitalist order that draws together political elites, the bureaucracy, industrialists, and the security/military community; is nationalist in orientation; and participates in the global economy on its own terms, as Imperial Germany and Imperial Japan did? During the 1980s and 1990s, Western commentators were confident that China's eventual, and not very distant, democratization was a foregone conclusion. More recently, however, many China experts have become less sure.[11]

China and Russia are very different, of course, but they may both represent a return of authoritarian-capitalist great powers absent since the defeat of Germany and Japan in 1945. Unlike Germany and Japan, China is the largest player in the international system in terms of population and is experiencing spectacular economic growth, which has been averaging 10 percent annually for 30 years. By shifting from communism to capitalism, China has switched to a far more efficient brand of authoritarianism. Starting from very low levels of wealth, China's per capita gross domestic product (GDP) is still only $4,000-$5,000 in purchasing power parity (or PPP), or between one-eighth and one-tenth that of the developed world. Yet, judging by the earlier dazzling development of other East Asian "tigers" (all of which China dwarfs), China's swift growth is expected to continue (even if at a decreasing rate) until it drastically narrows or even closes the economic gap with the developed world, thereby becoming a true nondemocratic superpower.

Naturally, all the old questions resurface regarding the viability of a different course to modernity from the liberal democratic one. Given the size of China and Russia and the balance of nuclear power, it is unthinkable that either will be crushed in war as were Germany and Japan. The central questions focus on their economic and political viability. These cannot be answered with any certainty because they involve counterfactuals about past occurrences, unknowns about future developments, and a small sample of cases that are heavily affected by contingency. But the issues can be clarified. The first step is to broaden our historical perspective by tracing the causes and consequences of the rise of capitalism and liberalism during modernity.

2
The Ascent of Capitalist Parliamentarianism

Both modern democracy and industrial capitalism developed from the liberal parliamentarianism and large-scale commercial capitalism that were inaugurated in Europe during early modernity. Commercial capitalism and liberal parliamentarianism were intertwined, and generated greater wealth and power than did competing systems at that time. In consequence, capitalist-parliamentary states increasingly gained a leading position within Europe and global ascendancy. This chapter will explore the link between capitalism, parliamentarianism, wealth, and power.

Europe as the Global Hub

This is not the place for a systematic discussion of what set in motion all the above developments in Europe from very humble beginnings sometime before the year 1500. From Montesquieu on, every major historical and social thinker—Voltaire, Hume, Adam Smith, Herder, Hegel, Marx, and Max Weber are only the giants among them—posited and variously attempted to explain Europe's special course, the so-called European Miracle or Rise of the West.[1] Notably, inter- and intra-state pluralism was greater in Europe than in the other centers of civilization, and that in turn owed a great deal to Europe's peculiar geography and ecology.

One of the distinctive features of European history compared to that of Eurasia's three other zones of dense sedentary civilization—Southeast Asia, India, and China—concerns imperial unity. In both Southeast Asia and China, imperial unification on a massive scale was achieved early in their histories, and thereafter became the norm, with only relatively brief relapses. Even in India, empires that encompassed most of the subcontinent alternated with periods of fragmentation. By contrast, Europe was never united by force from within, nor was it conquered from outside. Rome, the only arguable exception, was a Mediterranean, rather than a European, empire and incorporated only southern Europe. Moreover, while enduring for centuries and being highly influential, it lasted for only a fraction of European history. All other attempts at imperial unification—the Carolingian, Ottonian, Habsburgian, and Napoleonic—were geographically even more confined and short-lived.

Montesquieu, who identified this European uniqueness the earliest and defined it most clearly, discerned the geographical and ecological factors that underlay it:

> In Asia one has always seen great empires; in Europe they were never able to continue to exist. This is because the Asia we know has broader plains; it is cut into larger parts by seas; and, as it is more to the south, its streams dry up more easily, its mountains are less covered with snow, and its smaller rivers form slighter barriers. Therefore, power should always be despotic in Asia . . . In Europe, the natural divisions form many medium-size states, in which the government of laws is not incompatible with the maintenance of the state . . . This is what has formed a genius for liberty, which makes it very difficult to subjugate each part and to put it under a foreign force . . .[2]

Southwest and East Asia, and the north of the Indian subcontinent, incorporate large open plains, which facilitated rapid troop movement and imperial communications. By contrast, southern-western-central Europe is highly fragmented by mountains and sea. Sheltered behind these obstacles and benefiting from individual access to the sea, the many smaller political units that emerged in this fragmented landscape were able to defend their independence with much more success than those of Asia.

Greece is paradigmatic in this respect. Being Europe's most fragmented peninsula, crisscrossed as it is by mountains and sea, Greece foreshadowed in miniature the political fragmentation of the peninsular and rugged continent as a whole. More than coincidence, memory, and cultural transmission connected the Greeks to later European history. Of course, this does not mean that Europe could not possibly be united by force or conquered from outside, that its political fragmentation was somehow "deterministically preordained." It simply means that, rather than being wholly accidental, this fact of European history rested on physical and ecological conditions that made the consolidation of large political units on the continent that much more difficult, and a multiplicity of medium-size states its modern norm.

Smaller political scale was generally less conducive to the concentration of autocratic power and the corresponding decline in influence of both the aristocracy and the populace. Such a development took place in Asia once vast empires formed there: the so-called oriental despotism. Other geographical-ecological factors also contributed to Greece's, and later Europe's, political fragmentation and wider distribution of power. Western Europe was not exposed to a vast pastoralist steppe frontier, as China and even northern India were. Nor was it internally divided into arable and more arid, pastoral strips and zones, as was the case in Southwest Asia. In temperate Europe, rainfall was sufficient nearly everywhere for agriculture, so separate herding subsistence economies and herding societies barely existed. Thus western-central Europe was nearly free from the specter of raids and takeovers by nomadic mounted archers that were a prominent feature of the other centers of Eurasian civilization throughout history.

Furthermore, Europe's rainfall patterns also allowed dry rather than intensive-irrigation farming, so settlement was spread out rather than being densely concentrated in river valleys. This subsistence-settlement pattern had political consequences. As Montesquieu, Weber, and others have noted, irrigation agriculture was more conducive to autocratic rule.[3] In the first place, large irrigation systems necessitated communal organization and construction work, whereas practitioners of dry farming were more independent. Second, irrigation cultivators were much more vulnerable to the destruction of their livelihood by a force that might disrupt the irrigation system. Third, highly intensive cultivation of small irrigated plots left less time for other activities than did dry farming. As a consequence, irrigation cultivators tended to be more servile than dry-farming agriculturalists.

In comparison to the civilizations of Asia, these geographical and ecological patterns helped make the southern-western-central European interstate system more fragmented, and state-societies smaller, less polarized in terms of class and wealth, and less oppressive. Conversely, Asian societies were relatively more susceptible to imperial rule, more despotic, and socially and economically more polarized. It was precisely Europe's political division that enhanced its competitive edge.

Although large political blocs undoubtedly offered some advantages, such as fostering economic complexity and technological innovation, these advantages were regularly offset by the existence of monopolistic and despotic central authorities and stifling imperial administrations. Europe's political disunity, along with the greater power distribution within its states, made it more difficult for rulers to politically suppress innovation. Moreover, the penalty for suppressing an innovation could be its adoption by a rival state, giving the latter an advantage in the intense economic and military inter-polity competition that prevailed in Europe.

Geography and political plurality were also central to the establishment of a European trading system around 1500 that for the first time in history encompassed the entire globe, connecting the various continents via the oceans. This constituted the single most important factor in the shaping of modernity and was the true engine of the "European Miracle." It transformed Europe's society, economy, and states. Markets grew to play an unprecedented role, granting some European states greater resources, and hence greater power, than other states, while making Europe as a whole increasingly wealthy and more powerful in relation to other parts of the world. The emergence of a global trading system became the prime catalyst for the formation of capitalism in Europe. Ultimately, these developments stimulated industrialization, and a quantum leap in wealth and power.[4]

We can only briefly address this intriguing question: why was it Europe, rather than any of the other civilizations of Eurasia, that connected expanding inter-regional trade systems into the first global system? Other regional networks had been as advanced as Europe's, if not more so. Arab and Muslim merchants dominated the Indian Ocean. Great imperial Chinese fleets comprising huge multi-mast sailing ships were led in the early fifteenth century (1405-1433) in great naval expeditions by the eunuch admiral Cheng Huo, sailing as far as East Africa.[5] The lateen, triangular sail originated in the Indian Ocean, and the compass in China. And yet it was the Europeans who fully mastered the world's seas and reached the East, rather than the other way around.[6]

Asians had less incentive to carry out such long-range sea voyages because they were geographically more centrally placed and because the poorer European markets offered little attraction for them. Europe's disadvantages thus proved to be a spur to development. On the other end of Eurasia, China's leaders had good reason to feel that their rich and sophisticated civilization already possessed everything they needed. After Cheng Huo returned from East Africa in 1433, the Ming Dynasty's rulers decided to dismantle their advanced fleet of ocean-going junks and banned further long-range voyages. These state-funded voyages had been costly and their rewards dubious. Nor was long-range naval activity allowed to proceed in private hands and along more commercial lines because the despotic Chinese state, with its Confucian mandarin bureaucracy, disliked and suspected trade, traders, and independent capital. Therefore, the Portuguese met with little effective resistance at sea when Vasco da Gama burst into the Indian Ocean in 1498. And when Christopher Columbus, in the service of the Spanish monarchs, crossed the Atlantic en route to East Asia and stumbled onto America in 1492, the natives could offer little effective resistance on land. Thus Europe's ocean-going capability led to an extra, unexpected huge prize. Within a few years the world had opened up for European exploration and profit.

The question remained as to *which* Europeans in a pluralist and highly competitive state system would reap the advantages of that success—economically and, consequently, also politically and militarily. Although the pre-industrial European economy remained predominantly agrarian, mastery over markets on a global scale and a growing manufacturing sector that prospered by virtue of that mastery became a very significant source of wealth, of a more liquid sort than previously known. The sheer unprecedented scale of the global trading system transformed power relations between and within European societies more than any previous commercial supremacy ever had. The states that won out in the contest for domination over global trade secured the resources that made them strong in the European power struggle. And it was the traders' states that were best equipped to win the global trade contest.

Earlier in history, power had brought wealth, while wealth had translated into power more equivocally. But from about 1500 on, wealth and power were becoming increasingly interchangeable.* Before modernity, too, wealthy civilizations were able to pay for and sustain larger and better-equipped armies than their poorer neighbors on civilization's barbarian frontier. But this was an ambiguous advantage, for the barbarian frontier neighbors too often compensated for their poverty by superior ferocity and by relying on improvised logistics, living off their enemy's land. They repeatedly took over the wealthiest states and empires whose power had waned. The Mughal conquest of northern India from Afghanistan in 1526, and the conquest of China in 1644 by the Manchurians, can be regarded as the last instances of such recurring takeovers from the march. Henceforth, however, as Adam Smith observed, the balance between the civilized and the barbarian changed fundamentally.[7] Success in war became critically dependent upon military hardware—above all firearms—that required an advanced technological infrastructure to produce and a highly organized socio-political infrastructure to deploy effectively. No longer was there such a thing as a poor strong power. For the first time in history, only the wealthy qualified for the league of the mighty, with an almost uninterrupted loop between wealth and military prowess developing where previously an ambivalent relationship, if not a self-destructive cycle, had existed.

Thus, in order to survive, power had to serve the interests of the producing and trading economy, and the more it did so the more power was generated. Any shackles on the creation of social wealth

---

* This interrelationship is the main theme of Paul Kennedy's *The Rise and Fall of the Great Powers: Economic Change and Military Conflict from 1500 to 2000* (New York: Random House, 1988). But, indeed, it *only* applied as directly and unequivocally as it did after 1500.

by the state's political and military elite only undermined the power of that elite in competition with other states. For the first time in history, parasitic warrior states and warrior elites fell behind economically productive states and elites in terms of *power*.

Mastery over global trade and a prosperous manufacturing sector enhanced states' taxation efficiency in a number of ways. A comparison of the national wealth of Britain and France during their eighteenth-century struggle indicates that because France's population was about three times greater than Britain's, and agriculture was still the largest sector of the economy, the French economy was more than double the size of Britain's.[8] And yet Britain won the naval/military contest by virtue of its superior financial capability. The more liquid financial resources of Britain's far more commercialized economy constituted the key to its success.[9]

Moreover, the trading states excelled in developing deficit financing, raising low-interest loans in the new financial markets and successfully servicing a large national debt, which proved to be the key to their success in war. Previously, in order to finance war, states had sold public property, most notably land, and spent money treasured by the state and in temples. They could also squeeze capital from private hands through more or less arbitrary means. Merchants everywhere were an obvious source of disposable capital, though they were more defenseless in the despotic East. Yet seizure of capital had its disadvantages. Heavy levies imposed on merchants could kill the goose that lays the golden eggs. The merchants could be brought to ruin, lose their business to foreigners, or take it elsewhere. Furthermore, where property rights offered no security against an ever-present threat of arbitrary confiscation, economic activity was inhibited and money was driven into hiding, hoarded, and thereby taken out of circulation. Unlimited power to dip into people's pockets constituted an almost irresistible temptation. Thus it was in states where political power was limited, most notably because the rich ruled the state or were powerful enough to safeguard property rights, that a different avenue—loans—emerged to tap accumulated private capital for public spending, predominantly on war.[10]

Republican Rome offers a prime example. Massive mobilization during the protracted and ruinous First and Second Punic Wars exhausted the Roman state. To pay for the wars, the state doubled and tripled the "extraordinary" property war tax that it levied on its citizens (*tributum*), sold public land, and used the sacred emergency treasure. But in addition, during great crises, it borrowed money from the wealthy citizens, most of whom belonged to the leading senatorial class.[11] Of course, in one of the most successful war-making states ever, the Roman elite were not only paid back their money but were also the direct beneficiaries of the fruits of war. Rome's wars thus constituted an excellent investment. Things were more ambiguous in the commercial republican city-communes of Renaissance Italy and Germany. Financially advanced, they developed the system by which the huge cost of war was spread over the peace years through loans and through selling bonds that would be paid back with interest. However, the strategy of borrowing capital was employed in lieu of levying direct taxes that would have fallen mostly on the rich and which the municipal elite were reluctant to pay. Public debt spiraled and annual interest payments took up a substantial part of the cities' expenditures. As the financial burden mounted because of the cities' losing struggle against the rising territorial states, the system broke down.[12]

Indeed, borrowing was a slippery road with its own dangers, which the new European states did not escape. There was a great temptation to default on the payments in difficult times. The kings of Spain repeatedly defaulted—in 1557, 1560, 1575, 1596, 1607, 1627, 1647, 1652, 1660, and 1662—ruining the Fugger family banking house of Augsburg, the richest in the world, among many others. The French monarchy did the same in 1558, 1564, 1598, 1648, and

1661. But defaulting on payments backfired no less than direct confiscation, ruining not only the bankers but also the state's credit. Loans became more scarce and carried higher interest rates to compensate for the greater risk. A vicious spiral was created.

The early modern European state also resorted to another source of credit: the selling of offices, both civil and military. Individuals' cash investment in the purchase of office was earned back through regular state pay over the years, as well as from the opportunities for profit offered by the embezzlement of public money. Here, too, the easy temptations of credit created a vicious spiral of costs for the state, coupled with inefficiency. Not only was the state's administrative machinery corrupted by the need to raise money, but the ever-increasing sale of "venal" offices for that purpose also inflated the number of office holders beyond any functional need. As with any credit snowball, massive repayment costs in the form of salaries ultimately swallowed the proceeds from the system, leaving behind only its all-pervasive negative legacy.[13] Easily borrowed money was obtained by mortgaging the future. Like any leveraged investment, this was a high-risk, high-gain affair. A Darwinian race for credit fueled armed competition among the powers. All pushed borrowing to the limit and beyond, building up massive debts.

In this hazardous balancing act, seventeenth-century Spain and eighteenth-century France found themselves overburdened with ruinous debts they were unable to service. The Spanish debt in 1623 spiraled to 10 years of royal receipts.[14] Powers like Spain, whose credit status deteriorated, ultimately lost out in the military and naval race. In the French case, the financial crisis ultimately brought down the monarchy and the *ancien régime*, even though in absolute terms, France's debt only amounted to some 60 percent of Britain's. In relative terms, the French debt burden was smaller still, for it equaled just over half of France's GNP, whereas Britain's debt was almost twice its GNP.[15] Yet in seventeenth-century Holland and eighteenth-century Britain, deficit financing formed part of a winning package. Flourishing trade was the key: it created great financial wealth and a sophisticated money market, where new instruments such as stock exchanges and a national bank were used to float massive loans, spreading market principles and expanding the investing public.

Interest rates on state borrowing fell to as low as 2.5-4 percent in Holland and Britain, roughly half those France paid to its creditors, and perhaps a third to a sixth of the average historical price of credit to states.[16] The British national debt leaped upward with every war during the eighteenth century, rocketing to a staggering 20 times Britain's average annual tax income after the American War of Independence, or about twice its annual GNP. Between half and two-thirds of Britain's tax income was spent annually on (low) interest payments to service the debt, which paid for 30-40 percent of its spending during the wars.[17] Britain was the ultimate winner in the leverage race only because victories gave it a colonial empire and a commanding position over global trade, which in turn boosted its home economy in a period of substantial economic expansion. Wealth paid for war, while war laid the foundation for greater wealth creation. Thus the wealthy and economically more efficient won out. There was much more to the story, however.

Market Regimes

Rich markets and sophisticated financial tools comprised only one element in a wider political-economic system. The high financial credibility of the Dutch and British states reduced the risk of default on payment and lowered interest rates, while lower interest rates in turn increased the states' credibility. But underlying that high credibility was the fact that rather than constituting an alien body, the state served the interests of the mercantile economy, and, indeed, was largely controlled by the mercantile classes who dominated its powerful representative assemblies. Not only did strong representative governments in seventeenth-century Holland and eighteenth-century Britain provide greater security against default; the represented elite were willing to pay higher taxes in order to finance wars that served their interests. A broader tax base and increased income made it possible for the Netherlands and Britain to raise larger loans, which they were able to service and repay more easily.

Throughout history, the greater the incorporation of social groups into the state and the bigger their stake, the greater was their commitment; the more alien the state and its aims, the less voluntary support could it expect. As Montesquieu observed in *The Spirit of the Laws* (pt. 2, bk. 13, especially chap. 12), the freer the state, the more taxes it was able to levy. The Netherlands and Britain were the most heavily taxed, while absolutist France had lower tax revenues for its size, and the despotic Ottoman Empire was the most lightly taxed. An earlier generation of historians emphasized the greater taxing power of the new centralized absolutist state in comparison to feudal fragmentation. Yet more recently, scholars have become more aware of its power limitations. To overcome resistance to the concentration of political sovereignty, the crown had to compromise with local power, privileges, and institutions. These compromises, which resulted in tax exemptions and an uneven tax burden, caused serious inefficiencies in the state's money-raising system.[18]

Thus the representative-inclusive state regime was stronger and more able to generate and harness social resources or "infrastructural power" than the seemingly despotic absolutist state. If early modern European states variously taxed an estimated 5-15 percent of national income, Britain's wartime taxation crossed the 20 percent threshold in the eighteenth century, two to three times the per capita taxation of France, and four times what its own taxation level had been before the Glorious Revolution of 1688.[19] As with the Dutch Republic, this was partly due to Britain's superior commercial wealth. Still, "no (heavy) taxation without representation" turns out to have been more than a North American revolutionary slogan.

The representative institutions that emerged in the Europe of the late Middle Ages broke the rule that had prevailed earlier in history, according to which large states were necessarily despotic. As they gained strength, the monarchies of some of the states succeeded in rolling back the power of the assemblies during early modernity, becoming more despotic. However, in other European states the national assemblies held their own and grew to dominate. These states thus combined the freedoms and participation of small polities with the large size of a country-state.[20]

New information technology in the form of the printing press facilitated this development. It created what social historian Benedict Anderson has labeled "imagined communities": large-scale bodies of people who, although experiencing no face-to-face interaction as in small traditional communities, partook of a shared world of culture and ideas. This much-enhanced means of cultural transmission and communication greatly reinforced both national identity and the potential for cooperation on a national scale. Other civilizations, where hegemonic empires prevailed, again offer illuminating comparisons and contrasts to Europe. Although both paper and block printing were invented in China, the absence of an alphabetic script with a small number of letters hindered the development of movable type. Furthermore, China's state rulers and mandarin establishment (and the authorities in Tokugawa Japan) had no particular interest in facilitating the mass diffusion of ideas. The same applied to the world of Islam, where the Ottoman rulers banned the new technology.[21] In this, too, Europe's political fragmentation and pluralism prevented obstruction of the new invention and censorship of its products to the extent that took place elsewhere in Eurasia. Martin Luther and other Protestant reformers reached a wide public by using printed vernacular. The transmission of both the scientific revolution and the Enlightenment was no less intimately tied to printing.

It was predominantly the literate who were connected by printing into large-scale "imagined communities." Country gentlemen and town burghers were now brought up on a shared diet of classical and modern books. Moreover, they were increasingly informed about national current affairs by an ever-growing volume of pamphlets (from the sixteenth century), newsbooks (from the seventeenth), and journals and newspapers (from the eighteenth). And it was precisely these people who spearheaded the English, American, and French Revolutions.[22]

In the rebelling North American colonies, for example, the press that informed the townsfolk about the unfolding events and debated the political issues served as a major catalyst for the emerging national American identity, bridging the deep divisions that had separated the colonies. Furthermore, the founders of the republic were infused with the ideology of the Enlightenment, disseminated through the medium of the book. Thus wider political participation became possible in modern country-states not only by virtue of representatives who went from across the country to the capital, as the authors of the *Federalist Papers* (nos. 9, 14) pointed out, but equally because of the much greater availability of information traveling in the opposite direction.

Participation meant that the state had to become much more attuned to the wishes and interests of the represented, rather than serve the ambitions of autocratic rulers; the represented became effective rulers, and the state's business became their own, and vice versa. The cardinal question, then, is who they were. In Poland, for example, only the aristocracy was represented in the *seym*, while the burghers were excluded. In this aristocratic "republic," where the monarchy became elective, the landed aristocracy's social dominance and regional autonomy constituted the overriding consideration. Representation thus bred extreme decentralization of power, which ultimately made that once-powerful country easy prey for its neighbors. By contrast, in the United Provinces, the assemblies (States) were dominated by the commercial municipal oligarchy, which cooperated, not without great strain, with the princely *Stadtholders* of the House of Orange.

England is the most intriguing case, for it was dominated neither by the aristocracy nor by the merchants. As in other large "territorial" states, both lords and burghers sat in its national representative assembly, the Parliament. However, these estates' interests contrasted less than was generally the case elsewhere in Europe. That is because a momentous transformation took place in England, changing the relationship that had prevailed earlier in world history between the two main methods of wealth acquisition: forceful extraction and productive creation, of which the former had usually dominated. To be sure, the English social-political-military nobility did not give up its power, but rather transformed in response to the great attraction of the vastly expanding markets. As Adam Smith has observed, this historical transformation took place from the late Middle Ages on, when feudal lords in England found it more profitable to produce for a burgeoning manufacturing and trading urban market on a national and Western European scale, than to live off rent extracted from serf peasants (which inhibited a rise in productivity).[23] They then moved on to participate directly in that market as it expanded globally. Scale was the key to the process. The larger the market economy grew, the more profitable it became in comparison to small-scale, largely autarkic agricultural lordship, and the more it lured members of the aristocratic elite. Crossing the line that had traditionally separated aristocrats from merchants, aristocrats turned from rent extractors into full-fledged commercial enterprisers.

The English elite thus became more interested than anyone else in the country's commercial prosperity and more ready to invest in it militarily. This process turned England into the leading European trading nation and the spearhead of modernization. As Marx pointed out, the new economic-social-political regime was still based on massive coercion by the commercialized aristocratic-bourgeois elite, who enforced the regime on the non-represented populace through state and law.[24] All the same, Marx maintained that the capitalist, market economy differed from earlier forms of social organization in being geared towards production and because its extraction mechanism was predominantly economic, rather than based on the direct use or threat of violence.

Whereas in some European states commercial profiteering became a more promising avenue to wealth than forceful extraction, in relations among states, violent conflict remained fully intermixed with economic competition. Throughout history, traders strove to monopolize resources and markets by force if they were powerful enough to do so, rather than share them in open competition. Now, however, the game assumed global dimensions. Rivals were denied access to home markets by regulations and tariffs, and were directly pressured by war with the intention of weakening them, forcing them into commercial concessions, and banishing them from colonies and foreign markets. Labeled mercantilism, this commercial-military complex became the prime driving force behind the incessant wars of the seventeenth and eighteenth centuries.[25] In the seventeenth century, the Netherlands took over Portugal's trading empire in the East, and expanded its control over bulk trade in European waters. But later, two much larger and stronger powers, France and England, challenged the Netherlands' trading supremacy. In the eighteenth century, Britain emerged victorious from its contest with France, driving the French out of Canada and India and establishing itself as the foremost naval and trading nation.

The military and naval race obviously constituted a tremendous waste of resources. In addition to the massive devastation and loss of productivity, war and debt servicing caused by war comprised the largest single item of state expenditure during early modernity, ranging from around 40 percent in peacetime to 80-90 percent during the frequent wars. Between 1500 and 1750, each of the European great powers engaged in war more than 50 percent of the time.[26] Scholars have debated whether or not this "waste" ultimately proved economically beneficial because of the spinoff effects of large state investment in metallurgy, mining, shipbuilding, and supply.[27] But more significantly, war was integral to the historical process in which more productive market economies triumphed over traditional economic-political regimes. The European and global penetration of the market economy was made possible and was much hastened by the close interaction of economic success and military superiority. Thus early modern war carried a huge dividend in terms of economic development. Indeed, because of the strong interaction between wealth and power, states were driven to make themselves economically more productive in order to stay competitive in the great-powers race, no less than the other way around. For this purpose they undertook economic, social, and political reform.

We have already reviewed the examples from Western Europe, where the market economy famously went hand in hand with representative government and political liberalism. Developments in the Netherlands and England precipitated those in France, where the combination of a growing market economy and irresolvable war financing and debt crisis eventually brought about the revolution. However, the new great powers that emerged in Central and Eastern Europe during the eighteenth century—Prussia and Russia—were neither global maritime traders possessing advanced financial markets, nor representative and liberal regimes. Both these powers were autocracies that ruled despotically and often ruthlessly, imposing centralization, levying taxes, and raising large armies. Their first steps toward modernization actually involved greater coercion, the suppression of assemblies, and deepening enserfment of the peasantry within an absolutist (neo-)feudal-estates state.

And yet in Russia and Prussia, too, economic, social, and political modernization were the necessary preconditions of power. Whereas in England the agent of both economic modernization and increased national might was a wealth-seeking commercialized social elite, power-seeking autocratic state rulers were the agents of both these processes in Russia and Prussia. Where a commercialized social elite was absent or weak, "enlightened despots" were taking the lead in driving their countries to modernize—cultivating industries and other economic ventures, establishing state bureaucracies, and drawing on foreign expertise and capital. They thereby sought to create the tax base and manufacturing infrastructure that would allow their states to qualify for the great-powers league. Time and again in the subsequent centuries, it was above all the spur of the great-powers struggle that would propel these states to initiate new waves of reform, so as not to fall hopelessly behind. Economic and social modernization was enforced on them through the medium of war, rather than generated voluntarily from within. Growing modernization necessarily drove them into intractable domestic tensions and contradictions. It undermined the authority of the autocratic regime and the traditional agrarian elite that ruled these societies, forcing them to incorporate wider segments of society into the state in order to remain competitive in the economic and military race. Market regime was not merely an economic concept but also a social-political-military one.

Thus the modernizing reforms initiated by the Hohenzollerns in Prussia and by Peter the Great and his successors in Russia gained new momentum in the wake of Prussia's defeat by Napoleon's national mass armies (1806) and Russia's defeat in the Crimean War (1853-1856) by the industrial-military might of Britain and France.

Soon after, the same processes began to affect China and Japan.[28] The growth of capitalist market economies and national mass participation would never have succeeded as sweepingly as they did without the impetus of inter-state power politics, first in Europe and then throughout the world. Markets in themselves could not have prevailed had they not also generated superior force, as wealth and power became interchangeable.

The increasingly participatory civic-national European state turned into a *res publica* in the ancient Roman sense, where state power became "impersonal," public resources were separated from the private wealth of leaders and subjected to closer scrutiny, and the rule of law prevented arbitrary state action. Whereas earlier, "patrimonial" states had been tools in the hands of their rulers, the modern state progressively became identified with providing public services.

While these developments decreased "despotic power," they greatly enhanced states' "infrastructural power" by deepening social mobilization.[29] Furthermore, as regimes gained greater public legitimacy and enjoyed a wider social support base, and as lawful and peaceful means for changing government became available, violent usurpation decreased and domestic political stability increased. This evolution reflected the old virtues of mixed regimes, originally identified by Aristotle and his disciples and now expanded to a national scale through representative institutions and print technology. European states increasingly freed themselves from the specters of regicide and imbecile hereditary rulers that haunted traditional autocratic states and regularly threw them into periods of chaos or inaction.

Deducing from historical experience as interpreted by the wisdom of the ages, Enlightenment thinker Adam Ferguson[30] and many others after him, down to U.S. President Richard Nixon, feared that the growing wealth and prosperity of their civilized societies eroded

civic and military virtue and bred softness and decadence, which au-
gured eventual downfall. But Ferguson's contemporary and friend,
Adam Smith, saw that modern societies had outgrown the threat of
a military takeover from the barbarian frontier. Furthermore, although luxury and comfort continued to tempt members of established elites away from a life of action, in increasingly competitive
systems there were always economic and political upstarts who
moved in to take the lead.

By the eighteenth century, even before industrialization, Europeans had grown about twice as rich in per capita terms as their con-
temporaries in Asia,[31] and their more effective socio-political
structures gave them an extra edge. Whereas firearms could be successfully assimilated by the traditional empires of Asia, a highly developed market economy could not. During the first two centuries
of their presence in Asia, the Europeans had been far too weak to
challenge mighty China of the Ming and Manchu dynasties, India's
Mughal Empire, or Tokugawa Japan. Europeans had been tolerated
on the margins only because these empires were decidedly continental and inward-looking. The Ottoman Empire was the only Asian empire that bordered on Europe, and it exerted heavy military pressure
on Europe for centuries. By the eighteenth century, however, the Ot-
tomans and other Asian empires found themselves falling behind Europe in wealth and power.

In India, the decline and disintegration of the Mughal Empire
in the early eighteenth century made it possible for the British East
India Company—a state-like capitalist organization employing up-
start officials and generals—to step in as the new overlord. Europeans
were powerless to make inroads into China until well into the nineteenth century. Nonetheless, although industrialization during that
century is rightly cited as the crucial advance that allowed the West
dominance over China (and Japan), pre-industrial, national European
armies of the Napoleonic era were already far superior to any outside

Europe. The Mamluk and Ottoman forces proved to be no match for Napoleon's expeditionary army during his 1798-99 campaign in the Levant. Only China's huge size and distance sheltered it (and Japan) from European intervention for a further short while.

A Republican-Commercial Peace?

Armed mercantilism made European states increasingly powerful. However, if a much-expanded trading economy and a global market made it domestically more profitable for both the socially powerful and the state to release and ride on, rather than interfere with, the operation of market forces, the same logic should in principle have prevailed internationally. This was the idea that increasingly gained currency during the Enlightenment.[32] As Adam Smith argued in *The Wealth of Nations* (1776; bk. IV, chaps. vii-viii), mercantilism might give powerful countries a *relative* economic advantage over others; but by dividing international trade along political lines, it decreased *overall* wealth, lessening the absolute prosperity of the leading mercantilist countries themselves. Mercantilism reduced economic competitiveness and international economic specialization and exchange, which were the true engine of greater efficiency, productivity, and innovation. Smith's free trade doctrine was developed by David Ricardo, espoused by the Manchester School in the nineteenth century, and has since been championed by economic liberals as a recipe for both prosperity and peace.

However, in contrast to the domestic realm, the international arena was anarchic. There was no sovereign who monopolized power and was able to safeguard the rules of competition, thereby securing the players against those who might resort to violent conflict. Smith himself (bk. IV, chap. ii, sec. 23) conceded that considerations of the balance of power might legitimately impose constraints on free trade, for "defence . . . is of much more importance than opulence." If monopolizing markets allows a nation to achieve a relative advantage over others, why would it risk that advantage by opening markets to all to increase absolute wealth—which could allow a challenger to become richer and use its relative advantage to fight the former leader into ruin?

Britain, in fact, experienced such a power shift. During the eighteenth century, Britain had become the mercantilist economic-naval-imperial leader. In the nineteenth century, while further increasing its relative economic advantage with industrialization, Britain withdrew from mercantilism, opened its markets to foreigners and foreign goods, abolished protectionist tariffs, and lifted restrictions on investment and the sale of technology abroad, eventually becoming a free-trading state. Thereby it boosted its own growth while fueling that of the rest of the world. Yet in relative terms, this open policy made it easier for others—above all the United States and Germany—to catch up and eventually overtake Britain economically and to challenge its position as the mightiest power. Free trade may indeed lessen the motive to amass and use force to gain access to economic opportunity, but it can only securely be exercised if a state is confident that others will not resort to force for their own economic or other purposes. In a Hobbesian, anarchic, international system with no sovereign regulator, how can such confidence exist?

During the eighteenth century, Enlightenment thinkers addressed the question of how war could be eliminated, grappling with the problems of anarchy and the modern world. In his *Projet pour rendre la paix perpetuelle en Europe* (1713), Abbé de Saint-Pierre proposed an alliance of all the European rulers, who would together impose a general peace by deterring and punishing those who threatened to infringe on it. Assessing Saint-Pierre's program, Jean-Jacques Rousseau argued that autocratic rulers could not be trusted to carry it out because they would never forfeit part of their sovereignty or their hopes of foreign aggrandizement. Only a revolution that would rob the princes of their power might give hope for such a peace project.[33]

Republican proponents of the Enlightenment, like the Marquis de Condorcet in France and Thomas Paine in the United States, voiced this growing belief. As Paine put it in *The Rights of Man* (1791): "If universal peace, civilization, and commerce are ever to be the happy lot of man, it cannot be accomplished but by a revolution in the system of governments. All the monarchical governments are military. War is their trade, plunder and revenue are their objects."[34] "Why are not republics plunged into war," he added, "but because the nature of their Government does not admit of an interest distinct from that of the Nation?"[35] Moreover, he wrote, commerce "is a pacific system, operating to cordialize mankind, by rendering nations, as well as institutions useful to each other."[36]

Immanuel Kant expressed very similar ideas in his *Perpetual Peace* (1795). He, too, suggested that as the states developed constitutional-republican regimes, people would tend not to vote for war because they themselves would have to shoulder and pay the price for it. Constitutional-republican states should then federate, he continued, in order to resolve their differences peacefully.[37]

Kant wrote his book amid the general but short-lived enthusiasm among Europe's intellectuals for the French Revolution. But as the authors of the *Federalist Papers* (no. 6) had pointed out in rejection of the pacific view of republicanism, a glance through history would have taught Kant and Paine that some participatory republics were among the most bellicose and militarily successful states ever. This applied not only to direct democracies (like ancient Athens), which Kant believed lacked constitutional restraints and exercised a tyranny of the majority; it also applied to other Greek and Renaissance city-state republics and above all to mixed-regime republican Rome. The more the people held political power and shared in the spoils of war, the more enthusiastically they supported war and imperialism and the more tenaciously they fought. Furthermore, when Kant was writing his book, France's revolutionary wars could reasonably be viewed as defensive, a reaction to military intervention by the powers of the *ancien régime* who sought to extinguish the people's newly gained liberties. Soon, however, Revolutionary France took the offensive, and its mass citizen armies swept through Europe, subjugating it under French imperial domination.

Smith, Paine, and Kant wrote just before the beginning of a new epoch. In the following centuries, industrialization would generate resources and energies of Promethean magnitude, creating unimagined forces of destruction and unleashing "total" wars. How illusory, then, were the above thinkers' predictions and prescriptions, and what links in the causal chain did they miss?

3
Free Trade or Imperialism?

The Industrial Revolution, which took off in late eighteenth-century Britain, constituted a quantum leap in history. It sparked a steep and continuous growth in per capita production, marking a dramatic break from the "Malthusian trap" that had thus far characterized human history. Earlier productivity increases had been largely absorbed by population growth, leaving the vast majority of humanity in dire poverty, precariously close to subsistence level. With the outbreak of the industrial-technological revolution, however, that changed dramatically. In the developed countries, per capita production has increased by a factor of 15 to 30 since the outbreak of the revolution, more or less in the same range as the developed world's advantage in production over today's least developed countries (some of which are actually poorer than eighteenth-century Western Europe). The gap between the richer and poorer countries increased tenfold over this period. Average growth in the industrial world became some 10 times faster than in pre-industrial times, with production per capita for the first time registering substantial and sustained real growth at an average annual rate of 1.5-2.0 percent.[1]

The Decline of War

The industrial-technological revolution and the exponential growth in wealth in the affected countries radically transformed society, politics, and war. While the war-making potential of industrial countries rocketed in tandem with spiraling wealth, the number of wars and war years among the great powers and among economically advanced states in general decreased dramatically after the onset of the industrial era. In the century after 1815, they declined to about one-third of their frequency in the eighteenth century, and even lower compared to earlier times. The same reduced frequency continued during the twentieth century, although resource and manpower mobilization in the major wars that did occur (and, hence, wars' intensity and lethality per time unit) increased, most notably in the two World Wars.[2]

What accounts for this decline? Do the greater economic and human costs of the wars and their greater intensity and destructiveness explain the decline in the number of wars and war years among economically advanced societies? Many assume that wars simply became too expensive and lethal, with a tradeoff of sorts between the intensity and frequency of warfare: fewer larger wars replaced many smaller ones. This hypothesis barely holds, however, because relative to population and wealth, wars did not become more lethal and costly than they had been earlier in history.[3] Particularly during the nineteenth century, the occurrence of war in the developed world sharply declined, even though the wars that did occur were far from devastating, compared with earlier or later times. No great-power war occurred for 39 years after Waterloo—the longest peacetime in European history until then. The ensuing Crimean war (1854-1856) was limited, while the Franco-Austrian War (1859) and wars of German Unification (1864, 1866, 1870-71) were relatively short and inexpensive. All the same, these wars were followed by another record: 43 peace years among the European great powers between 1871 and 1914.

Conversely, in the twentieth century, the mere 21 years separating the two World Wars that were the most intense and devastating in modern European history do not suggest an inverse relation between war intensity and frequency either. Indeed, all specialized statistical studies of the subject reject the idea of any such relationship.[4] Obviously, when great-power wars did come, the antagonists were able to throw much greater resources into them. At the same time, however, they proved reluctant to embark on such wars in the first place. A third consecutive record followed World War II: more than 60 years without war between economically developed countries. Although this "long peace" is often attributed to the nuclear factor—a decisive one to be sure—the trend had been evident long before the advent of nuclear weapons. By far the three longest periods of peace in the modern great-powers system have occurred since 1815.

It is unlikely that this development owes nothing to the simultaneous onset of the industrial-technological age. How, then, might the two developments be related? This question has been around since the nineteenth century, approached with more or less skepticism, depending on the times, but thus far the answers have never crystallized into a satisfactory and comprehensive explanation.

Clearly, the fundamental and novel development of the industrial-technological age was rapid and continuous growth in real wealth. No longer was wealth a finite quantity about which the main question was how to divide it. Wealth acquisition was progressively changing from a zero-sum game, in which one participant's gain could only be achieved at another's expense. In economically advanced countries, economic rather than predatory activity became the main avenue to wealth (which poor countries became too weak to win through conquest). Furthermore, national economies were no longer overwhelmingly autarkic and therefore barely affected by one another; they were increasingly connected in an intensifying and spreading network of specialization and exchange—the much-celebrated "globalization" of markets and the economy. Prosperity abroad became interrelated to prosperity at home, whereas foreign devastation potentially depressed the entire system and was thus detrimental to each country's well-being. Contemporary thinkers clearly recognized the radical novelty of this relationship. As John Stuart Mill put it:

> Commerce first taught nations to see with good will the wealth and prosperity of one another. Before, the patriot, unless sufficiently advanced in culture to feel the world his country, wished all countries weak, poor, and ill-governed, but his own: he now sees in their wealth and progress a direct source of wealth and progress to his own country. It is commerce which is rapidly rendering war obsolete.[5]

To be sure, this did not guarantee harmony. Economic relations remained competitive—indeed they grew ever more so. All the same, the greater the yields brought by competitive economic cooperation, the more counterproductive and less attractive conflict became. Although many believe that conflict declined because war was becoming costlier, in fact it was peace that was growing more profitable. The influential social thinker Auguste Comte (echoing his mentor Henri de Saint-Simon) expressed the growing belief in the first half of the nineteenth century that warrior society was giving way to the industrial stage of human development.[6]

Nineteenth century progressivists shared this belief, and it seemed to account for the very real decline in wars in Europe's economically advanced areas. However, in the wake of the two twentieth-century World Wars, nineteenth-century optimistic economic pacifism lost its credibility, at least for a while. What, then, were the theory's flaws? Where did a generally valid economic rationale prove deficient?

We may begin by examining the great powers' wars that disturbed the nineteenth century's relative peacefulness. Apart from the

Crimean War (1854-1856), these were the War of 1859, which led to Italy's unification, the American Civil War (1861-1865), and the Wars of German Unification (1864, 1866, 1870-1871). What were these wars about? Above all, issues of national unity, national independence, national self-determination, and national identity constituted the deepest and most inflammable motives for these major wars. The same held true for violent conflict in general throughout Europe.[7] The hotspots of conflict were fueled by nationalism: conquered and partitioned Poland, fragmented and foreign-dominated Italy, disunited Germany, the territories of the future Belgium briefly stitched to Holland, suppressed Ireland, Habsburg-incorporated Hungary, Ottoman-held Balkans, and Alsace-Lorraine, annexed to Germany but retaining their affinity for France. Thus the rising tide of modern nationalism that engulfed Europe during the nineteenth century often overrode the logic of the new economic realities.

The Puzzle of Empire

Nationalism was also a mediating factor in other potential causes of violent conflict. Great-power imperialism in the industrially undeveloped parts of the world was probably the major cause of conflict and mounting international tensions in the generation before World War I, and was largely responsible for the outbreak of both World Wars. In addition, imperialism was central to relations between the industrially developed and undeveloped worlds, and spurred a large number of colonial wars. Between 1878 and 1920, the European powers carved up the world among themselves. In 1800, Europeans already controlled 35 percent of the world's land surface, including colonies and former colonies. They increased their control to 67 percent in 1878, and 84 percent in 1914. In 1800, the British Empire, the largest power of them all, possessed a land area of 1.5 million square miles and a population of 20 million. During the following century, it expanded sevenfold in area and twentyfold in population. After World War I, it encompassed 23.9 percent of the world's land surface.[8]

What accounts for this new spate of imperial expansion and how did it stand in relation to the economic rationale described above? This is a much-debated topic that has engaged commentators, ideologues, and scholars. As with any historical phenomenon, a variety of factors contributed to the new imperialism. But it may best be understood within the context of the two general developments that underlie modernity: the rise of a Western-dominated industrial world economy and the corresponding surge in Western technological-military prowess—the explosion of wealth and power.

Indeed, one reason imperialism took off is that it became so easy.[9] Technological innovations during the nineteenth century made the penetration and domination of hitherto inaccessible territories far easier for the powers of the developed world. Steamboats were able to go up rivers into the depths of landlocked countries and continents, from China and Indochina to Africa. Quinine provided an effective medicine against the highly lethal malaria. The rifled, then breach-loading, then magazine-fed infantry gun gave Westerners an unprecedented superiority in firepower over the people of the undeveloped world. The railway and the telegraph connected vast occupied territories, making them far easier to control than they had been. This was true not only for Asia and Africa but also for North America, where the conquest of the West was greatly aided by the new technologies of firearms and communications. As the technological-industrial gap between the developed and undeveloped parts of the world opened up, so did the inequality in power between them.

However, ease does not explain motivation. Why go in at all? Imperialism was not a new historical phenomenon, of course. Did the new wave of imperial expansion during the industrial age differ from earlier empire-building? Throughout pre-modern history, tribute extraction, agricultural colonization, and trade benefits had been the principal material rewards of imperial expansion. During the European expansion in the early modern period, trading posts and the monopolization of trade grew in significance, as global trading became the engine of Europe's increasing wealth. Although Adam Smith rejected the economic logic of protectionist monopolization and colonialism, it was only in the industrial age that Britain embraced free trade.

Greater freedom of trade became all the more attractive in the industrial age for the simple reason that the overwhelming share of fast-growing and diversifying production was now intended for sale in the marketplace rather than for direct consumption by the family producers themselves, as had been the case in the pre-industrial economy. Lower barriers to the flow of goods enhanced the efficiency of the exploding market economy.[10] During industrialization, the European powers' foreign trade increased twice as quickly as their fast growing GNPs, so that by the late nineteenth and early twentieth centuries, exports plus imports grew to around half of GNP in Britain and France, more than one-third in Germany, and around one-third in Italy (and Japan).[11] Greater freedom of trade was the corollary to the vast expansion of the market economy in the industrial age. This certainly held true for the world's industrial leader, Britain, whose manufactured goods were likely to win against any competition during its mid-Victorian zenith. According to free-trade economic theory, colonies were at best irrelevant to wealth acquisition, and often detrimental to it, because of the resulting political interferences with the operation of the markets. Aggregate size of a country, and hence also its imperial possessions, do not matter economically if free trade prevails; people's (per capita) wealth bears little relation to their country's size.

All this, however, only holds if free trade prevails. For this reason, free trade did not eliminate imperialism but rather created "The

Imperialism of Free Trade," as a seminal, controversial article by John Gallagher and Ronald Robinson was titled.[12] During the nineteenth century, Britain used its economic and military power to negotiate with and coerce foreign political authorities to secure free trade, or at least low tariff barriers, for British goods. Although the British did not request preference over other powers, they were positioned to gain the most from the lifting of trade restrictions. Gunboat diplomacy was occasionally employed to achieve this objective. As Marx memorably wrote:

> "The cheap prices of [capitalism's] commodities are the heavy artillery with which it batters down all Chinese walls, with which it forces the barbarians' intensely obstinate hatred of foreigners to capitulate. . . . It compels them to adopt what it calls civilization into their midst."[13]

True, but Chinese walls first had to be battered down by the advanced armies and navies of capitalist societies before capitalist goods were allowed in to do their work. And the penetrated societies could not forge any effective military counterforce before they undertook domestic economic-social-political modernization. Superior economic and military power were related, and they reinforced each other in transforming traditional societies, which accelerated capitalist expansion worldwide. Cheap goods alone could have been blocked out politically by traditional elites apprehensive of change.

According to Gallagher and Robinson, the British created an "informal" empire in South America, the Middle East, East Asia, and parts of Africa, where a nominally sovereign yet variably dominated periphery—economically and politically—maximized economic profit for Britain while minimizing the costs of intervention, conflict, and direct rule. Formal empire figured only as the last resort, when informal, hegemonic imperialism had failed. This nineteenth-century British-dominated global economic-political sphere became archetypal of "free-trade imperialism," which would be associated with the United States after World War II.

Critics of the Gallagher-Robinson thesis have stressed that the British government was intensely reluctant to get involved in the internal politics of foreign countries and had very limited influence on their affairs, casting doubt on the political domination and "informal empire" notion.[14] It is generally agreed, however, that as Britain embraced free trade in the middle of the nineteenth century, its use of coercive power changed from that which it exerted during the era of monopolistic trade and monopolistic empire:

> "Willingness to limit the use of paramount power to establishing security for trade is the distinctive feature of the British imperialism of free trade in the nineteenth century, in contrast to the mercantilist use of power to obtain commercial supremacy and monopoly through political possession."[15]

Moreover, one should add that the imperialism of free trade differed from the older tributary imperialism (elements of which obviously lingered on) in that its underlying rationale was not extraction, but mutually beneficial trade, generating growing wealth and the whole range of attendant benefits *for all*. Although historical tributary empires, too, often professed to bring peace, stability, and the blessing of civilization to their subjects, informal liberal imperialism constituted a radical departure from the past to the degree that the industrial takeoff itself constituted a radical departure. To be sure, the process was anything but ideal. The Opium War (1839-1842), which forced China to open up to the British export of that drug, is a glaring example of the process's many abuses. Furthermore, capitalism's "creative destruction," in Joseph Schumpeter's phrase, involves painful transformation and dislocation as a matter of course, and all the more so for traditional, pre-industrial societies. Still, connecting others to the world economy—whether voluntarily, through pressure, or even through force—was their only road to sustained growth and away from the material deprivation, stagnation, zero-sum competition, and high mortality of the premodern world.

The rhetoric of anti-imperialism has all too easily swept this fact aside.[16] Indeed, it was for this reason that J. S. Mill looked favorably on imperialism when conditions were right. The vision of general progress guided not only liberal theorists but liberal statesmen everywhere. In the mid-nineteenth century, British Prime Minister Lord Palmerston believed that in the Ottoman Empire, a thriving trade would

> bring the Sultan to introduce liberal reforms which would give the subject peoples representation in government and property rights in the Courts. The productive classes were to be freed from the exactions of their quasi-feudal Moslem overlords whose rule, the British believed, had kept the country backward and poor for centuries. Once liberated, the peasant would produce more for the market, the Oriental merchant would accumulate capital and his enterprise would develop the economy in partnership with the British merchant. The flowing trade would spread liberal notions of justice and freedom.[17]

By this logic, Britain's pioneering path to modernity would be replicated everywhere because the pressure of low-cost goods from the already modernized core would automatically generate similar processes throughout the world's pre-industrial periphery—or would be aided by force where necessary.

Spreading industrial globalization indeed proved irresistible (and on the whole highly beneficial materially), yet not quite along the lines envisaged by liberals and by Whig notions of progress. Since it was formulated by Adam Smith and David Ricardo, the theory of free trade has withstood most challenges, and the vast majority of economists today embrace it; yet a few major exceptions and some nagging questions remain. The principal exception concerns those countries whose social and political infrastructures were developed enough to facilitate an industrial "takeoff." However, as "national economists" in these countries—from Alexander Hamilton and Friedrich List on—pointed out, their nascent industries needed the protection of tariff barriers in their home markets against the products of more established industrial economies, at least until they developed sufficiently to be able to compete successfully. During the nineteenth and much of the twentieth centuries, the gap in the standard of living between the economically advanced and less advanced countries was not yet as wide as it is today, and therefore the latter did not enjoy far lower labor costs that could compensate them for the leaders' industrial advantage. Thus the United States, Germany, France, Russia, and Japan all adopted strong protectionist policies against British manufacturing during their own period of industrial takeoff in the late nineteenth century. Contrary to liberal orthodoxy, no major country ever became a first-class economy without first embracing protectionism. In these developed parts of the world, there was no question of Britain's exerting pressure—let alone military pressure—to enforce free trade.

The imperialism of free trade worked best in less developed countries, where local elites could be successfully drawn into the British-dominated world economy in a mutually-beneficial yet asymmetrical relationship. These countries mostly exported foodstuffs and raw materials to Britain, while importing British manufactured goods. Only rarely, in times of crisis—when the local political authorities and elites who were involved in (and guaranteed the safety of) foreign business lost control—might a short-term armed intervention be initiated to restore order and the economic interests of the hegemonic power, Britain or any other.

There was, however, a third category of countries—most notably China and those of Islam—where the combined pressure of low-cost goods and gunboat diplomacy from the developed world met with deep-seated local resistance to change. Exposure to the Western global economy and Western-induced modernization undermined the indigenous and more traditional political-social-economic-cultural order. State authorities proved inept or weak; state bureaucracies, stifling and corrupt. Among those who stood to benefit or lose from an economic transformation, it was the latter who held political power. Feudal and tribal elites were incapable of making the transition to the market that had been uniquely achieved by the British aristocracy—or were unwilling to do so; the merchant class was not allowed to grow sufficiently to become significant. Cultural attitudes strongly mediated against market-oriented reform, which was viewed as foreign intrusion. There was an even worse scenario. Failing to develop, native society also failed to compete economically and incurred foreign debt. National reaction against the foreigners followed, engulfing the populace, which experienced only the stresses of capitalism without its benefits. Tottering collaborative indigenous political authorities could not be restored by short-term intervention. Already-existing foreign interests were threatened. In these situations, the hegemon was faced with the conflicting options of either withdrawal or intervention to impose direct, formal imperial control. Contrary to the Gallagher and Robinson formula of "trade with informal control if possible; trade with rule when necessary," the latter option was rarely adopted for commercial reasons.[18]

The most notable exception was India, the jewel of the British formal empire. Britain acquired India by force during the era of monopolistic trading imperialism, and held onto it in the era of free trade-imperialism, partly because it had already been under British rule, but also because the liberal British authorities became convinced by the mid-nineteenth century that a withdrawal of formal imperial rule would harm both India and British trade. British officials feared that India would revert into the hands of exploitative, corrupt, and warring state rulers; efficient administrative and honest justice systems would disappear; social reform and economic development would stall; and both the masses of peasantry and the urban classes would be surrendered to their social superiors. Concomitantly, the British worried that anarchy and trade barriers would disrupt its trade with one-fifth to one-sixth of all humanity living on the Indian subcontinent. Thus a sense of duty born of liberal morality and self-interest reinforced each other in sustaining British rule in India.[19]

China was a different case. Unlike India, it did not constitute a British imperial bequest from an earlier age, and had limited susceptibility to the encroachments of free-trade imperialism. The problem was not the Celestial Kingdom's strength but its weakness. The British used gunboat diplomacy to open China to trade with the West, but the declining dynastic rule proved little inclined to, and little capable of, embracing change and reforming society and the economy. As a result, although encompassing nearly a quarter of humanity, China's value as a trading partner declined in comparison with the developing and increasingly richer parts of the world. The disastrous Tai-Ping peasant rebellion (1851-1864), the greatest bloodletting of the nineteenth century, exposed the weakening of China's central government. Concerned about the prospect of anarchy and unwilling to shoulder the burden of direct imperial rule over the huge kingdom, Britain viewed China's slow modernization and limited integration into the world economy as the least harmful of the available options.

Much the same applied to the Ottoman Empire, where market-induced social reforms and economic modernization again fell far short of liberal hopes. Nonetheless, only in Egypt did the collapse of the Khedive regime—whose failing modernization program and ensuing massive foreign debts generated strong nationalist and Islamic anti-Western revolutionary forces—prompt Britain to intervene in 1882. And temporary intervention turned permanent only when it became clear that withdrawal would leave behind no political power able to guarantee Western interests. The British takeover proved pivotal because it triggered the "scramble for Africa," which in as little as two decades would lead to the partitioning of the entire continent among the European powers.

This eruption of massive formal imperial expansion in Africa has been viewed as puzzling, because it seemed to make no economic sense. Anarchy or a hostile government in Egypt would have threatened existing Western financial and commercial interests, but the potential losses in themselves would not have persuaded William Gladstone's Liberal government to assume what the frustrated Gladstone termed a permanent "Egyptian bondage" that went against all its principles. Even more, the puzzle of imperial expansion concerned the vast sub-Saharan African territories—among the world's poorest, least developed, and least profitable—which promised very little for the imperial powers in return for the costs of administration, policing, and infrastructure. Gold-rich South Africa and rubber-rich Belgian Congo were African colonies promising real rewards, but they were rare exceptions. Then as now, the wealth of the developed world derived from home-based manufacturing and services and from trade with other developed and semi-developed countries. Then as now, formal or informal empires in Africa contributed exceedingly little to that wealth.

As the data for the world's foremost colonial empire and chief financier show, Britain made about 40 percent of its investment domestically during the late nineteenth and early twentieth centuries; another 45 percent went to the United States, South America, and continental Europe; and only around 15 percent went to the formal empire. Furthermore, investment in the empire overwhelmingly concentrated in the self-governing, white dominions: Canada, Australia, and New Zealand. The empire in India came next in the volume of investment, whereas investment in the new, least-developed African colonies was negligible. Furthermore, contrary to the famous thesis promoted by the British economist and publicist J. M. Hobson and adopted by Lenin, investors did not seek colonial markets in preference over diminishing returns on investment in the developed economies. The more developed the country of investment, the higher were the returns, with the new African acquisitions bringing the lowest returns. Trade data for France, the second largest imperial power, were similar.[20] The new wave of imperial expansion constituted a negligible business.

This is demonstrated by the fact that the fastest-growing economies of the late nineteenth century were the United States and Germany, which, despite their new colonial ambitions and minor acquisitions, were the least of the colonial empires (though obviously some of the U.S.'s meteoric growth came from its internal westward expansion across North America). Conversely, the largest and fastest growing colonial empires, Britain and France, suffered the greatest relative decline in economic status among the great powers during the era of the new imperialism.

Since the imperial powers recognized at the time that Africa offered only meager economic benefits, what brought the scramble for colonies? More than Africa was at stake. In the first place, there was the British empire in India. To secure the sea route from Europe to India, Britain had already taken control of South Africa. The British intervention and sojourn in Egypt were prompted mostly by a desire to secure the safety of the recently-opened Suez Canal, with its shorter sea route to India. Britain was especially concerned by Russia's advance in central Asia and its ambitions in the eastern Mediterranean. Thus neither of Britain's two major colonial possessions in Africa had much economic value in Britain's system of free trade; rather, they were intended to secure that system against other powers that might threaten British trade by military force. The British concern in the Transvaal was motivated not by its newly found mineral wealth but by the fear that this wealth would lead the Boers to reassert their independence and ally with Germany, which was now based in Southwest and East Africa. Yet, other powers could not but view British security-motivated actions as monopolization. Although India, for example, was open to trade with others, British administration there undoubtedly gave British economic interests preferential status. France, with its long-standing economic and political involvement in Egypt, thus regarded the British takeover of Egypt as a blow, both economically and in terms of prestige.

The scramble for Africa cascaded from that point. Incensed by Britain's continued presence in Egypt, France initiated a huge colonial expansion across the Sahara, connecting its Algerian and West African possessions. The motive for this move lay in the realm of national prestige rather than economics, and it was intended to pressure Britain to leave Egypt. In fact, it achieved the opposite. Fearing that France would control the Sudan, the upper Nile, and, hence, Egypt's water, Britain moved to bring the entire Nile Valley under its formal control, including the Sudan, Uganda, and the East African land route to Uganda (Kenya). The process of preemptive land-grabbing accelerated when Germany obtained its own colonies in Africa (1884-1885). Bismarck took them mainly for domestic political reasons, for he dismissed African colonies as irrelevant. The great powers handed the huge Congo territory to the king of Belgium as his personal possession because they deemed that preferable to its control by any of the other great powers.

Thus the scramble started with Britain's defense-motivated expansion, which in turn prompted a fear of monopolization among all the powers. Free-trading Britain increasingly regarded formal empire as a necessary preemptive policy, once other, protectionist, powers began to expand their own formal empires, which they would close to outsiders. Britain came to view formal empire as the best way to secure free trade, while for protectionist powers the preemptive aspect of the grab was at least as compelling. Either way, the result was a runaway process.

China was, of course, an incomparably more important economic prize than Africa, yet a similar dynamic had developed there by the late 1890s. With the progress of its Trans-Siberian railroad, Russia was for the first time becoming capable of military power projection onto China's frontier. Britain's naval supremacy was no longer enough to guarantee China's independence as an "open door" but British-dominated market. At the same time, other industrializing powers—Japan, Germany, France, and the United States—were increasing their presence in China. China's defeat in the war with Japan (1894-1895) further weakened its regime. The country's political disintegration now appeared imminent, heightening the competition among the great powers. A collapse of indigenous authority would most likely mean partition, and no power could afford to be left out. Although all the powers preferred a united and open Chinese market, each increased its encroachments on China's sovereignty, thereby triggering the process of partition. Regarded as an almost foregone conclusion in the closing years of the nineteenth century, partition was averted after Japan removed the threat of a Russian advance with its victory in Manchuria (1904-1905).

With partition taking place in Africa and looming over China, the British-dominated free-trade system was threatened by the prospect of protectionism, which was a self-reinforcing process and self-fulfilling prophecy. Britain's exports had already been suffering badly due to the high tariff barriers adopted by all the other great powers, as well as surging German and American industrial competitiveness that progressively blunted Britain's lead in foreign markets. As its position as the economic hegemon waned, Britain increasingly contemplated the advantages of retreating from free trade and consolidating its vast formal empire into a protectionist trade zone.

Championed by Colonial Secretary Joseph Chamberlain at the turn of the century and partly implemented in the wake of World War I, this policy was finally adopted in 1932, during the Great Depression. By contrast, it was now the United States and Germany that were increasingly interested in the removal of trade barriers to their manufacturing exports.

The United States, with its huge domestic market, was less dependent on foreign trade; yet the growth of global protectionism in the 1930s hit its exports the hardest and inhibited American recovery from the Depression. By the advent of the twentieth century, Wilhelmine Germans felt that only a "United States of Europe" free-trade zone or a European common market (and at the very least an economically unified *Mitteleuropa*) would offer German industry sufficient scope to develop, comparable to the vast spaces of the United States, the British Empire, and Russia. Furthermore, if the emerging global economy were to be geographically sliced among the powers rather than open to all, Germany, too, would require a large colonial empire, most likely in central Africa (*Mittelafrika*). With World War I and Germany's subsequent defeat, these designs grew more militant and extreme. For Adolph Hitler, the creation of an economically self-sufficient German Reich that would bestride continental Europe was inseparable from his racist plans and vision of a perpetual global struggle. All the inter-connected aspects of the liberal program were replaced by their antitheses.

Much the same would hold true for Japan. Lacking raw materials and heavily dependent on trade, the erection of protectionist walls by the other great powers hit Japan hard in the early 1930s. During the following decade, Japan increasingly regarded the establishment of its own self-sufficient empire, the so-called Greater East Asia Co-Prosperity Sphere, as essential to its survival.

Here lay the seeds of the two World Wars among the great powers. If the industrial-commercial global economy was to be partitioned rather than open, the pressure to grab territory became irresistible. From this perspective, it mattered little that turn-of-the-century Africa was of scant economic value, because its long-range prospect for development as part of a global colonial empire was more important. Furthermore, the Germans viewed the spread of the English-speaking peoples and culture as an enviable model, regarding the empire as a future destination for German immigration. Japan viewed its own empire in similar terms. Thus national considerations—always paramount—were further boosted as the free-trade model of the global economy was giving way to protectionism, and consequently also to imperialism and power politics. In a partitioned global economy, economic power increased national strength, while national strength defended and increased economic power. National size made little difference in an open international economy, but became the key to economic success in a closed, neo-mercantilist international economy dominated by power politics.

With the coming of the twentieth century, free-trade liberalism was in retreat not only because of the mutual fear of protectionism but because it was increasingly regarded as fundamentally flawed. The market economy was losing public favor, as its volatility, waste, and social costs were criticized, and progressives, fascists, and socialists alike advocated the virtues of planning and regulation. Politically too, the parliamentary-liberal and progressively more democratic model of mass society was being confronted by new, formidable totalitarian ideologies and regimes.

4
The Return of the Nondemocratic Great Powers

Liberal-parliamentary Britain was the first industrial nation, having been a pioneer of commercial capitalism during early modernity. There was a close connection, discussed earlier in this book and well-recognized at the time, between the political and economic aspects of its evolution. And during much of the nineteenth century, as Britain's epoch-making leap into modernity was transforming the world and commanding universal attention, its model constituted the paradigm against which all future development was judged. This paradigm inspired not only admiration and envy, but also deep apprehension and resistance, both within and outside the West. The disappearing virtues of traditional society were widely lamented, and contrasted with the alienating rule of mammon. Traditional agrarian elites and autocratic regimes feared the inevitable loss of power. Yet rejecting industrialization and its corollaries would mean falling hopelessly behind, not only in terms of wealth but also in inter-state power, as experienced by the Ottoman and Chinese empires, whose very existence became jeopardized. The Meiji reformer-revolutionaries in Japan summed up this realization in their slogan: "rich country and a strong army." As a result, conservative nineteenth-century European powers east of the Rhine, such as Germany, Austria, and Russia, as well as Japan and many others—

then and later—sought to embrace industrialization and carry out the necessary social and political reforms that went with it, while also preserving as much as possible their autocratic-aristocratic regimes and traditional values.

The old elites acutely felt the inherent tensions, if not contradictions, of this approach and these made them pessimistic about the success of their "rearguard" action. The agrarian aristocracy was a declining estate that could not survive into modernity. But whether traditional regimes could have adapted sufficiently to survive in powerful and advanced industrial societies such as Germany, Russia, or Japan, without necessarily adopting the liberal model cannot be told; because this historical experiment was interrupted by defeat in war and by the rise of totalitarianism that mainly replaced conservative autocratic/oligarchic regimes in their home countries. Rooted in modern developments, the new totalitarian regimes claimed to be more in line with modernity than either old conservatism or parliamentary liberalism.

The Twentieth Century's Totalitarian Alternatives

In either its left- or right-wing form, totalitarianism was a distinctively new type of regime, different from earlier historical autocracies and only possible with the advent of the twentieth century. It was rooted in what people since the late nineteenth century saw as the defining development of their time—one we now take for granted: the emergence of "mass society." The term mass connoted popular concentration, interaction, and mobilization, rather than numbers, because multitudes of peasants had always existed in all societies. However, they were impotently dispersed through the countryside, like potatoes in a sack, in Marx's phrase. Out of sight and out of mind, they were incapable of pulling their weight together and were totally disenfranchised, except in city-states. With industrialization and urbanization, all this changed. As the populace crowded into the cities, they were located near the centers of power and political authority, which could no longer ignore them. Henceforth, any regime had to be a "popular" regime, in the sense that it had to derive legitimacy from one form or another of mass consent. As a result, old liberal-parliamentarianism was itself transformed. Historically suspicious of the masses, apprehensive that political equality would threaten individual liberty and private property, and limiting the franchise to the propertied classes, it was now obliged to democratize. Gradually expanding during the nineteenth century, the franchise became a near universal norm in liberal-parliamentary societies by the 1920s. Liberal democracy came into being, a hybrid that was almost as novel as the totalitarian regimes emerging at the same time.

Advancing communications of the nineteenth century—newspapers, railroads, and the electric telegraph—had already given rise to popular plebiscite autocracy on a nation-wide scale, akin to the popular brand of tyranny that until then had been mostly limited to city-states. Pioneered by Napoleon I but exemplified by Napoleon III in France, it was labeled Bonapartism or Caesarism. In the twentieth century, newer breakthroughs in communication technology further enhanced mass society, even in countries that lagged behind in urbanization. Cinema and newsreels joined the popular press as a means of disseminating ideas, and by the 1920s, radio helped reach into remote corners of a country. The telephone and the automobile gave police a similar reach. The ability to control and harness mass education and mass media and to suppress all opposition to a degree never before seen gave the new totalitarian regimes unprecedented control over both public and private spheres. They thereby achieved high levels of material and spiritual mobilization, in contrast to traditional despotism.[1]

Indeed, while massive and ruthless terror was central for achieving social mobilization and obedience, terror alone was never sufficient for generating the sort of fanatical commitment exhibited by totalitarian societies. A sweeping popular ideological creed was indispensable in firing up the masses, in eliciting the sense of participation in something that concerned them directly and deeply, without which true mobilization has never been possible. Comprehensive ideologies of virtue and salvation—secular religions of conflicting brands—now largely replaced or supplemented older religious ideologies. On these grounds, both left- and right-wing totalitarianism, each led by an avant-garde party elite, successfully claimed to be more truly representative of the people than parliamentary liberal democracy. Each advanced a sweeping alternative to liberal democracy with respect to the question of how the new mass industrial society was to be structured.

Communism rejected both the market system, with its social inequality and antagonistic social relations, and liberal parliamentarism, which it regarded, even in its democratic forms, as a thin disguise for the actual rule of capital. It projected a salvationist vision based on social ownership and social planning that would liberate people from both material want and spiritual alienation. This was a most powerful mobilizing creed. Yet, if only because the realities of communist regimes fell so short of the ideal, all communist regimes in times of crisis successfully invoked indigenous nationalism (which they had ideologically and officially dismissed) as the supreme mobilizing agent.

Nationalism was, of course, the dominant theme of right-wing totalitarianism. While retaining capitalism, right-wing totalitarianism aimed to recast it as a radical antithesis to liberal society. Right-wing totalitarianism, too, represented nothing less than an out-and-out reaction and revolt against what were widely regarded as the ills of the liberal model: rampant capitalism; endemic social strife; divisive party politics; erosion of communal identity and sense of common purpose; alienating egotistic individualism; shallow materialism, lack of spirituality, and the disenchantment of life; vulgar popular culture, humanitarian weakness, and decadence. Within the right-wing totalitarian model, capitalism was to be efficiently regulated, the poor were to be provided for and disciplined, and a cohesive national community was to be created, infused with a sense of brotherhood and purpose—both domestically and against outside rivals. A cult of violence, belligerency, heroic sacrifice, and perpetual struggle for domination was cultivated, most notably in 1930s Germany and Japan, where a traditional warrior ethos and deep-rooted resistance to West European humanitarian liberalism had long been central to the national makeup.

As we saw in chapter 1, the gigantic three-way clash of the twentieth century ended with the victory of the democracies. The communist powers turned out to be economically inefficient and dismantled themselves peacefully. By contrast, the capitalist authoritarian and totalitarian powers, whose economies were no less efficient than those of their liberal rivals, were defeated in war primarily because they were too small.

As capitalism and liberalism were closely connected during early modernity, it is necessary to clarify what this connection included and what it did not. The emergent liberal regimes had at their core the transfer of political power into the hands of the commercial classes that worked to establish the market and capitalist activity against resistance from a number of quarters: part of the old agrarian aristocracy that did not commercialize (in Britain it mostly did); the masses of peasantry who were losing their livelihood in the face of the new and far more productive commercialized agriculture; and the masses of workers who were being forced to leave the countryside and flock into capitalist enterprises. The project was anything but democratic, as both the traditional peasantry and urban proletariat were rightly suspected of being hostile to a process whose rewards for them were very far off indeed. It took until late in the nineteenth century for the transformation to industrial capitalism to be completed, for the traditional agrarian sector to become insignificant, and for an empowered urban population to gain a stake in the system that steadily increased as the middle class expanded and affluence levels rose for the workers as well. Only then was the franchise expanded and democracy established in Britain.

The tension between development and democracy has since replayed itself in developing societies, most recently in the paradigmatic cases of China and India. Whereas nondemocratic China ruthlessly enforces capitalist reforms with little regard for the peasantry and industrial workers, generating record growth rates, democratic India's leap into modernity is slower because of the compromises that have to be struck with the peasantry that still constitutes the majority of the population.

Thus not only liberal-parliamentary but also authoritarian and semi-authoritarian regimes can pursue capitalist modernization as long as they give strong priority to commercial and industrial interests. Nineteenth-century Germany is a prime example of that process, having achieved record growth rates and overtaken Britain, despite some lingering influence of the old agrarian elite. In today's China, such an agrarian elite does not exist, and the regime's commitment to capitalist modernization is complete. Still, what happens after the modernizing project succeeds, society is transformed, and the urban masses are empowered? Does democratization not follow, as it did in Britain? It is widely believed that ultimately a lack of democratic institutions hinders capitalist development, while capitalist development undermines nondemocratic regimes. With the meteoric growth of China and Russia's retreat from liberalism and democracy, the whole subject again becomes highly relevant. We return to the question raised at the end of chapter 1: Are the new capitalist nondemocratic great powers viable?

The Challenge Resumed: Is Authoritarianism Compatible with Modernity?

We begin with the economic aspect. It is contended that un-free societies may excel in mass manufacturing but not in the advanced stages of the information economy that require an open and individualistic culture. As already noted, Imperial and Nazi Germany stood at the forefront of the scientific and manufacturing economies of their respective times. Japan was still behind the leading great powers in terms of economic development in 1941, but its growth rate, beginning in 1913, had been the highest in the world. This past record may be judged irrelevant to the information age; yet nondemocratic Singapore has a highly successful information economy. It is argued that Singapore is a city-state, rather than a giant country-state, but it is not clear which side of the argument this fact reinforces; urban societies and metropolitan centers of large countries are supposed to be the most susceptible to democratization pressures, yet Singapore is highly urban and economically advanced while remaining undemocratic. In China and Russia, their still relatively backward economic status means it will be a long time before they reach the stage where the possibility of a nondemocratic large state with an advanced capitalist economy can be tested.

Skepticism regarding the sustainability of Russia's oligarchic and kleptocratic capitalism is the most warranted. Critics point out that Russia's surge under Vladimir Putin has been built on the bonanza in the price of oil and gas, and is economically limited. Russia's per capita GDP rose from $2,000 in 1998 (very low) to $9,000 in 2008 (low-medium) in current exchange rates,[2] and the increase may already be proving temporary. Despite its new assertiveness and Western concern, Russia remains a poor and, on the whole, weak country, and is unlikely to break through to the rank of the advanced economies unless it is able to revive its manufacturing sector, building on its educated work force. This in turn requires secure property rights and a stable rule of law, something emphasized by the new President Dmitry Medvedev. Germany was semi-authoritarian until 1918, yet it had a very strong rule of law, as did Japan until 1945.

China is by far a more important and challenging test case than Russia. It is much larger, with about nine times the population of Russia, and its manufacturing-driven growth has been spectacular. Both big business and entrepreneurial capitalism are thriving there.[3] The question is whether they can continue to thrive once China moves into more advanced stages of development and loses the advantage of cheap labor. It is widely contended that because of a lack of political accountability and transparency, China will increasingly feel the ill effects of crony favoritism and corruption, already much in evidence today, as they are in most developing economies. In addition, a lack of individual freedom may hinder entrepreneurial and scientific creativity.

All these are cogent points, but perhaps less compelling than their proponents believe. The high scores that East Asian students regularly achieve in international tests are often contrasted with the greater freedom and intellectual agility of American students. Indeed, each cultural tradition may have its strong points. As for corruption, Singapore remains the sole existing example of a nondemocratic first-class economy, which continued to grow at a superior pace even after reaching a cutting-edge status (though it is badly hit by the current economic crisis). But as Alan Greenspan, the former chairman of the U.S. Federal Reserve Bank, writes, Singapore is one of the least corrupt states in the world[4]—as was Imperial Germany and its Prussian predecessor. It has become an axiom that corruption is inevitable in the absence of democratic transparency and accountability. Yet for Max Weber, Prussian-German bureaucracy became paradigmatic, and it was justly famous for its efficiency and clean hands. The secret of these model cases lies in the bureaucracy's high social status, strong ethics of duty and public service, and, in Singapore, high pay. Whether China's neo-mandarin regime can establish similar standards remains to be seen.

Furthermore, as Greenspan points out with a sense of wonder, Japan, too, has a very unusual and culturally distinct system by Western standards. Industry, finance, and government in Japan function as an intimate club that does not operate strictly along classical economic lines and is permeated with a strong collective spirit. Admittedly, Japan's long stagnation since its 1989 economic crisis is largely attributed to these distinctive traits, which in the 1980s were celebrated for contributing to Japan's staggering success. Accepted wisdom fluctuates widely over time, and it may adjust again following the great American housing and credit crisis that began in late 2007, coming after some 20 successful years during which the United States was recast as the world's economic role model. Like the markets, images and moods tend to overshoot. Moreover, even if we assume that a lack of political accountability in nondemocratic countries such as China might hinder economic performance, this problem may be offset by other advantages, including higher levels of social mobilization. And even with per capita wealth at the low end of the developed world's spectrum, which China is expected to reach in the 2020s, it will be a colossal power and far from the economic failure that the Soviet Union was.

If the economic argument is not as conclusive as many believe it to be, perhaps the socio-political transformation generated by economic development would cause eventual democratization. It is widely believed that economic and social development creates pressures for democratization that an authoritarian state structure will not be able to contain. After all, why would the people, once they become educated and affluent, agree to be ruled by a government they did not elect? Michael Mandelbaum, for example, argues that capitalism is synonymous with individual choice. People who become used to exercising consumer choice in every decision of their daily lives would begin to demand the same right politically. Thus nondemocratic capitalist regimes are based on an internal contradiction that inclines them to implode.[5] There is much truth in this argument and it appears very convincing—except that the world is full of contradictions and tensions that do not necessarily implode. As Mandelbaum and many others have pointed out, capitalist democracy itself is a combination that has always been torn between the great economic inequality generated by capitalism (which also biases the democratic political process) and democracy's overwhelming egalitarian drive.[6] This tension was so stark that socialists throughout the nineteenth and much of the twentieth centuries regarded it as an irreconcilable contradiction certain to doom capitalist democracy. As a result, they ordained socialism—economic democratization—as the wave of the future. In the meantime, some of the tension has been alleviated through the institution of the welfare state in capitalist democratic countries. Still, the tension has always remained very close to the surface, occasionally bursting out. People regularly live with tensions and contradictions, and the question is which of these prove to be more significant and irreconcilable.

Ronald Inglehart and Christian Welzel offer a value-centered version of the thesis that modernization leads to democracy.[7] They document clear differences between low- and high-income societies, with a shift occurring from the survival values of traditional societies and their emphasis on religion, respect for and obedience to authority, and national pride to individuality, self-fulfillment, and tolerant sexual mores in affluent, modern, and eventually postmodern societies. Drawing on twentieth-century experience, they reasonably argue that such transformation of values lays the groundwork for democratization. But like other varieties of modernization theory, theirs too overlooks the fundamental question at hand: Social values undoubtedly change with modernization, but are the modern values they record indeed an inevitable universal product of industrialization and greater affluence? Or has this particular set of values itself been decisively shaped by the overwhelming political, economic, and cultural liberal hegemony that the U.S. and the West have exercised since the destruction of the capitalist nondemocratic great powers—with their strong group values—in the first half of the twentieth century?

Inglehart and Welzel stress the persistence of different cultural traditions and significant cultural variations even among societies that have undergone modernization. It has yet to be determined whether genuine alternatives to, or significant variations on, the prevailing hegemonic values and socio-political system compatible with modernity arise and prove viable, most notably in East Asia, the world's most populous and fastest developing region.

Contrary to perception in the West, liberal democracy is not merely a neutral mechanism for choosing between values; it is itself an ideological choice, incorporating a whole set of values that many societies and cultures find to be deeply in conflict with other values they cherish more dearly. Some traditional values are incompatible with modernity and constitute an obstacle to the modernization of the societies that espouse them. But others may be more compatible.

Individualism has been the defining feature of the Anglo-American liberalism that emerged in the special circumstances of the westernmost parts of the West. Walter Russell Mead's *God and Gold: Britain, America, and the Making of the Modern World* (2007) covers this subject very well. There were other varieties of the democratic tradition, most notably French republicanism, which was strongly statist and centralist and laid much greater emphasis on the national collective. Yet these were more or less subsumed under Anglo-American individualist liberalism as it won dominance over the West. And there were of course the group-centered, nationalist traditions most prominently represented by nondemocratic Germany and Japan. We have already cited the early-twentieth-century sweeping critique of liberal democracy's perceived negative traits. With the defeat of democracy's rivals and the prosperity achieved by liberal democratic societies, public consensus in the West came to regard these traits either as inherently good or as the cost of a highly successful system whose virtues far outweigh its vices—a system, as Churchill put it, that is far superior to any other ever tried. Yet in other parts of the world people are less sure.

Many regard what they perceive as excessive individualism, universal egoism, and rampant hedonism, associated with Western liberalism, as a frustrating and ultimately unsatisfying creed. There is a widespread perception that this creed is rootless and nihilistic, and there is a great yearning for a thicker spiritual and communal way of life. In the past, such sentiments were in part responsible for fascism's great attraction and powerful spell, but this does not mean they cannot take more benign forms. Although liberal societies have been functioning tremendously well, a sense of cultural crisis or malaise has often accompanied them (and may be largely inescapable in societies that have met people's more pressing material needs). While individuals are always socially constituted, how to strike the proper balance between individual freedom and the claims of community is an enduring question.

Throughout East Asia, public sentiment favors "Asian values" over what it views as Western cultural imperialism. East Asia is one of the oldest centers of civilization, and its particular geopolitical conditions and historical trajectory gave rise to a greater emphasis on group values, social harmony, and hierarchy, usually associated with Confucianism, the region's dominant spiritual system. Many scholars are rightly suspicious of "cultural determinism," pointing out that from Max Weber on, Confucianism's traditionalism, conformity, and disdain for commercial pursuits were regarded as the reason for the failure of modernization in China, whereas more recently the Confucian emphasis on duty, learning, and hard work are widely cited as a major force behind the East Asian economic miracle. Cultures and social values are not immutable and are always transforming in response to changing conditions; nor, however, as the World Values Survey shows, are they insignificant "super-structures."

In looking for socio-political expressions of "Asian values," I shall pass over Singapore, whose former leading diplomat turned professor, Kishore Mahbudani, has recently published a passionate book, *The New Asian Hemisphere: The Irresistible Shift of Global Power to the East* (2008), that promotes Asian values and "Asian competence" against Western hegemony and "incompetence." Again, Japan is in some ways a more revealing example, precisely because it was so successfully democratized by the U.S. more than half a century ago. For practically the entire period of Japanese democracy, the same party, the conservative Liberal Democratic Party, has ruled the country. There was only one short break, between 1993 and 1996, when the party lost the leadership (returning as a junior coalition partner in 1994-1996). Absent this brief interruption, Japan would not have been counted by some measures that require at least one change of government as an indicator of a functioning democracy. Although dependent on electoral consent, Japan's ruling party has survived in power despite pervasive favoritism, periodic scandals, closed inner-circle politics, and national economic downturns. This record is very unusual by modern Western standards, and it would be hard to deny that it has at least something to do with the country's cultural traits. Japan's strong group values also place it among the least unequal societies in the world economically, along with the Scandinavian countries and other successful "deviants" from the standard capitalist form (though not developed Singapore or Hong Kong, and developing China).

To be sure, Japanese society continues to change rapidly, which somewhat erodes Japan's economic egalitarianism. An eventual change of government is also to be expected. Furthermore, Japan is very different from China—East Asian countries should not all be thrown into the same basket. Still, Japan historically is the most adaptive East Asian civilization and has been the most directly and thoroughly transformed by defeat and by American occupation. And if genuinely democratic Japan reveals so distinctive a difference from Western standards in its socio-political behavior, what might one expect from a country like China? What is to be expected from a country that is undemocratic, giant, unconquered and unconquerable, historically proud and self-centered, and driven in modern times by an overriding desire to revive its former glory and reassert its cultural self against hegemonic pressures from outside? From the time that China's rapid modernization began and until the democratic demonstrations that were crushed by brute force in Tiananmen Square in 1989, many Chinese intellectuals shared the prevailing Western belief that economic liberalization was bound to lead to democracy. But since 1989, the intellectual mood in China has changed a great deal. Liberals are becoming a minority, and not only because their views are being suppressed.

A defining feature of China today is that it is in a process of transition, indeed the beginning of transition, leaving behind a defunct and bankrupt communist system and looking for a way into a future that is not yet clear. In its own way, the same applies to Russia. Unlike Russia (which at least nominally remains democratic and possesses democratic institutions), China is still ruled by a communist party, the Communist Party of China (CPC), though in reality the party is no longer communist. The regime espouses a "third way" message, between capitalism and socialism, and is publicly committed to spreading wealth and social equality. As with all ideologies, this message is particularly appealing to intellectuals. But as noted above, the reality in China so far has been one of unrestrained modernization that resolutely quells unrest among the rural and urban poor.

Since the beginning of market reforms in the late 1970s, successful economic modernization and the maintenance of social stability have constituted the CPC's raison d'être and source of legitimacy. The Party is highly pragmatic and ready to adopt any measure that would sustain it in power and continue the process.

Without ideological legitimacy and a guiding ethos, no regime can stand for long, and China's official communist ideology is no longer believed by anybody. This is a critical challenge. Imperial Germany was a monarchy that drew legitimacy from both traditional sources and a long record of successful service; in Imperial Japan the emperor was sacred and the symbol of the nation; and the Nazi regime was legitimized by a messianic ideology and by the cult of the Fuehrer. Nondemocratic China has no traditional institutions that can claim the "mandate of heaven" of the Chinese emperors; nor is it likely to adopt a messianic ideology like communism or fascism. Fascism may have been more typical of societies in an intermediate phase of modernization, and could constitute a greater danger in Russia, where both economic development and the imperial legacy are more problematic, and evoke analogies with Weimar Germany. Nationalism is and will continue to be a central element of both China's and Russia's ideological moods. It will be promoted not only in the negative sense of a rebellion against the dominance of other cultures, but also in the positive sense of people looking for a source of identification with their society—grounded in people-hood and culture—that some feel is not sufficiently manifest in liberal democracies.

A possible ideology for China would emphasize Chinese ways, incorporate Confucian values of meritocratic-technocratic hierarchy, public service, social order and harmony, and be presented as a contrast to liberal divisiveness and individual irresponsibility. It has been dubbed mandarin rule without an emperor. Rejection of democracy in China stems not only from the regime's concern for its self-preservation but also from deep genuine skepticism regarding the merits of popular government. As during the 1930s, the recent economic crisis greatly reinforced this skepticism by diminishing democracy's image of success. To be sure, the idea of government by the wise and most qualified has as long a pedigree as democracy, and it is not limited to the Confucian tradition. It was also famously expressed by Confucius' near contemporary, Plato. The problems of rule by a self-electing elite have long revealed themselves in history. Most notably, there is the question of what will prevent the rulers from abusing power for their own good—or, as Plato's *Republic* compels us to consider, who will "guard the guardians"? Can China's ruling party escape this problem? Can it draw the most skilful into a meritocratic state hierarchy, rather than ossify into a rigid oligarchy? The history of such attempts is not encouraging. All that can be said at present is that China's regime is not a personal dictatorship of the more common authoritarian mold, and that forms of adaptation to the party's rule are actively sought.

Institutionally, the regime in China is continuously broadening its base, co-opting the business elite into the party, democratizing the party itself, and experimenting with various forms of popular participation, including village and some town elections, public opinion surveys, and focus group polling—all of which are intended to ensure that the government does not lose the public's pulse.[8] The internet is widely utilized in these experiments, as well as heavily and effectively censored.[9] As Fareed Zakaria has shown, the communications revolution—satellite, cable, and the internet—has brought about a massive expansion of indigenous cultural expression, even more than it has generated the parallel development of borderless globalization that has been widely assumed to spell the death of authoritarianism.[10]

Analyst Mark Leonard has labeled China's political and internet experimentation "deliberative polling" and "deliberative dictatorship." "Deliberative neo-mandarin party rule" may be a more accurate description of the regime. Indeed, the catalogue of possible options may be broader than the dichotomy of liberal democracy-authoritarianism. It ranges from a totalitarian turn of some sort to more pluralistic authoritarianism—incorporating various forms of participation and representation (as Imperial Germany and Imperial Japan variously did)—to illiberal democracy, in Zakaria's phrase. The Communist Party of China could also be replaced by another authoritarian or semi-authoritarian ruling body. Presently, the regime is treading cautiously and playing for time both at home and abroad. It is fearful of its own people and is deeply aware of its vulnerability and of China's still-relatively low levels of development. At the same time, it is also aware of the prospect that the country's meteoric development will give both China and the regime a far stronger hand within a generation. The regime's survival in whatever form hinges on that success. If China's road to modernity proves successful, there may be less need for an authoritarian regime that forces capitalist modernization on the rural and urban masses, and greater pressure for democratization by an affluent bourgeois society. Experimentation with limited representation and public deliberation could also create a dynamic towards democracy. Alternatively, successful modernization could bolster both the country and its regime through major gains in power, pride, self-confidence, and legitimacy.

There is also the question of what happens if there is a failure, in the intermediate future or beyond, with legitimacy remaining the regime's greatest problem. Totalitarianism profited from a galvanizing ideological message that, so long as it remained credible, legitimized great social mobilization and commitment. Authoritarian regimes are much shallower ideologically and have a much greater legitimacy problem. Nationalism is their most effective mobilizing tool. Nationalist sentiments are very strong in China (and of course in Russia), and the regime often beats the nationalist drums, though conscious that this dangerous tactic may get out of control.[11] In addition to a strong ideological message, totalitarianism relied on overwhelming terror. In today's China (and Russia), there is suppression of active opposition—sometimes harsh suppression—but no pervasive sense of terror, which may augur either well or ill for the regime.

According to Andrew Nathan of Columbia University, co-editor of a forthcoming study of how Asians view democracy, a survey in eight East Asian countries showed the highest public satisfaction with the regime in nondemocratic China. The other countries studied were five new democracies (South Korea, Taiwan, the Philippines, Thailand, and Mongolia), Hong Kong (actually a Chinese region), and democratic Japan, where satisfaction was lowest. The authors are not optimistic that China is on the brink of democratic change. They suggest it is "poised to join the list of developed countries with large middle classes and non-democratic regimes."[12] Admittedly, China's current levels of development are probably at least partly responsible for the results.

The most compelling argument I have encountered for the ultimate victory of democracy is the following: The record shows that while democratic regimes appear during modernity in countries at all levels of development, they may fall and be replaced by nondemocratic regimes in countries that are still in the early or intermediate levels of development (and vice versa). However, at high levels of development, democracy no longer loses power. It becomes virtually immune to overthrow, whereas this is not true of nondemocratic regimes.[13] It follows that although developed nondemocratic countries are possible, every change of regime from nondemocratic to democratic, as may occur from time to time, is one-directional in developed countries. In the long run, this will tend to reduce the number of developed nondemocratic countries until this category disappears. Is the record that suggests that developed democracies are not replaceable also a function of democracy's spectacular success and hegemonic status since World War II, and could change if a new nondemocratic and successful capitalist-developed Second World emerges? I do not know.

I am not a prophet and I do not pretend to predict whether or not China will eventually democratize and/or whether Russia will reverse its retreat from democracy. What I suggest is a different reading of twentieth-century history that is more contingent, less unilinear and less triumphant for democracy. It suggests that the democratization of major actors such as China and Russia—and hence the face of the future—is far from preordained. There is nothing in the historical records to show that the transition to democracy by capitalist nondemocratic powers is inevitable, whereas there is a great deal to suggest that such powers have a far greater economic and military potential than their communist predecessors.

The underlying question is whether liberal democracy is the only socio-political regime compatible with modern capitalist society, and whether there is only one viable road to, and one sustainable form of, modernity. This has been the central socio-political question of the modern era since the Industrial Revolution, and it remains without a definitive answer and may not be answerable definitively. Nothing, of course, is preordained or inevitable. All the same, ever since Britain's breakthrough to modernity, it has been widely believed that capitalist-industrial society and liberal democracy naturally go together and that there is a strong propensity for them to be linked. I do not deny that such a natural link or propensity exists and is largely responsible for the proliferation and success of liberal democracy during the past two centuries. Nonetheless, a propensity, even a strong one, is just that: whether it, rather than other, sometimes competing propensities, will be realized depends on circumstances, contingent events, and other imponderables. The wholly unexpected eruption of the global economic crisis in 2007-2008 offered a renewed reminder of, and warning against, our addiction to seemingly solid certainties in the face of reality's surprises.

This means that even if China and Russia eventually democratize, the cause of democracy's ultimate victory may be contingent rather than necessary. Nazi strategy has been described as a stepping-stone program, whereby each consecutive step of expansion was intended to secure the resources for further expansion, until Germany strode the whole of continental Europe, gained economic self-sufficiency, and became a world power. Although democracy's course was different in every respect, the stepping-stone model may explain a great deal of its successful expansion. There were some immensely lucky strokes at the root of that process. Britain's position as a large island close to but protected from continental Europe was a propitious setting for the growth of liberalism as Europe became the world's trading hub. Later, the Anglo-Saxon tradition was planted in the much more spacious and even more protected North American soil, and the giant liberal democratic United States emerged. As a result, while the West was gaining global dominance, the Anglo-American brand of individualistic liberal democracy was gaining dominance over the West. American might proved decisive in crushing and eventually democratizing the much smaller Germany and Japan, while the far larger China and Russia took the path of inefficient communist totalitarianism. Thus liberal democracy expanded momentously throughout the developed world, securing global economic, political, military, and ideological hegemony at the close of the twentieth century, and demonstrating its many blessings. So much so that the democratizing pressures on China and Russia may prove irresistible. Moreover, although the two powers will not necessarily be allies, the democratization of either of them, were it to occur, would leave the other more isolated and exposed. The resurgence of nondemocratic capitalist great powers may have come too late ultimately to be successful. Each link in the historical chain has been critical for the march of democracy, and a failure at any point could have resulted in a very different world, politically and ideologically.

For most practical purposes, it matters little whether democracy wins because of overwhelming intrinsic advantages and developmental imperatives or because of favorable contingent circumstances. But it does matter to scholars who seek to understand the most fundamental processes of modernity. And it matters practically for assessing how China and Russia may develop in the coming years—for the global triumph of democracy is not yet secured. Even if the capitalist nondemocratic great powers eventually democratize, the process could take decades or generations to unfold. Twenty-first century international relations could be dominated by different, and possibly opposing, systems.

The Global Balance

Although the rise of nondemocratic capitalist great powers would not necessarily lead to nondemocratic hegemony, open conflict, or war, it might mean that the near-total dominance of liberal democracy since the Soviet Union's collapse could be short-lived and that a universal "democratic peace" could still be far off. The new capitalist nondemocratic powers could be as deeply integrated into the world economy as Imperial Germany and Imperial Japan were, and not choose to pursue autarky, as Nazi Germany and the communist bloc did. With the possible exception of the sore problem of Taiwan, China is also likely to be less restless and revisionist than the territorially confined Germany and Japan were; although Russia, which is still reeling from having lost an empire, may be more problematic. The Russian intervention in Georgia in 2008 demonstrates this problematic potential. China still considers itself relatively weak and is mindful of the gap it needs to close in order to complete its modern-

ization. Until then, moderation and restraint in international relations is China's official policy, and it welcomes every veto power it
has in the system, which is why it is greatly in favor of multilateralism.
However, as China grows in power, it is likely to become more as-
sertive, flex its muscles, and behave like a superpower, even if it does
not become particularly aggressive.

China's free access to the global economy fuels its massive
growth, thereby strengthening it as a potential archrival, a problem
encountered by nineteenth-century free-trading Britain facing other
industrializing great powers. Fortunately for Britain, though, and for
democracy, British hegemony fell to another liberal democracy, the
United States, rather than to nondemocratic Germany and Japan.
With respect to China, one option might have been to make access
conditional on democratization. It is doubtful, though, that such a
linkage would have been advantageous or even feasible. Not only has
China's economic growth been highly beneficial to economic prosperity world-wide, making the developed world and the United
States in particular as dependent on China as China is dependent on
them; but economic development and interdependence in themselves—in addition to democracy—are also major forces for peace.
The democracies' ability to affect internal democratization in countries much smaller and weaker than China is very limited, and pressure could backfire, souring relations with China and diverting its
development onto dangerous paths.

Some commentators suggest that China's admission into the
institutions of the liberal international order built after World War
II and the Cold War will oblige it to conform and transform.[14] But
large players are unlikely to accept the existing order as it is, and
their entrance into the system is as likely to change it as to change
them. For example, the Universal Declaration of Human Rights,
drafted by Eleanor Roosevelt, Réné Cassin, and other dignitaries,
was adopted by the United Nations in 1948, in the aftermath of the

Nazi horrors and at the high point of American liberal hegemony. Yet the United Nations Commission on Human Rights, and the Council that replaced it, have long been dominated by China, Cuba, and Saudi Arabia, and have a clear illiberal majority and record. Similarly, in a reality unfamiliar since the end of the Cold War, more countries in the General Assembly of the United Nations now vote with China than with the United States and Europe on human rights issues. There are endemic and possibly irreconcilable dilemmas for liberal democracies here.

The democratic and nondemocratic powers may coexist more or less peacefully, albeit warily, side by side. They may be armed because of mutual fear and suspicion of each other—the so-called security dilemma—and against worst case scenarios that may not materialize. But there is also the prospect of more antagonistic relations, accentuated ideological rivalries, potential and actual conflicts, intensified arms races, and even a new Cold War, with spheres of influence and opposing coalitions. Although it is natural to look at the prospects through the prism of a few paradigmatic historical cases, future international patterns and great power relations will probably vary from those of any of the great twentieth-century conflicts, as conditions are never quite the same.

There need not be formal camps in the pattern of the Cold War in order for the new nondemocratic-capitalist model, if successful, to gain adherents. Even in its current bastions in the West, the liberal political and economic consensus may be vulnerable to unforeseen developments, such as a crushing economic crisis like the one that began in 2007-2008, that could disrupt the global trading system. Or there might be a resurgence of ethnic strife in a Europe increasingly concerned about immigration and national minorities. And if the hegemonic core is shaken, other parts of world—where adherence to liberalism and democracy, if existing, is recent, incomplete, and insecure—might be more deeply affected.

Southeast Asia and Latin America, as well as central Asia, the Middle East, and Africa, where development has yet to take off, are particularly susceptible to the capitalist nondemocratic model. (The concept of "bureaucratic authoritarianism" was originally developed in reference to Latin America.[15]) In many of these regions, Chinese economic involvement by way of trade, investment, and development is booming, and it comes with no strings attached, no requests to reform the domestic system, and no humanitarian criteria to meet. Even in the absence of formal camps, China is likely to encourage nondemocratic regimes that break the liberal democratic hegemony and make China itself appear less abnormal.

Critics argue that, unlike liberalism, capitalist authoritarianism has no universal message to offer the world, nothing attractive to sell that people can aspire to, and hence no "soft power" to win hearts and minds. But there is a flip side to the universalist argument. In the first place, many find liberal universalism dogmatic, intrusive, and even oppressive. Even in the West, most notably in the United States, there has been a conservative backlash against perceived excesses of liberal ideology, and in other cultures the threat perception is much higher. Resistance to a unipolar world concerns not only the power of the United States but also the hegemony of human rights liberalism. There is a deep and widespread resentment in non-Western societies to being lectured by the West, and to the need to justify themselves by the standards of the hegemonic liberal morality that preaches individualism to societies that value the community as the greater good.[16] Capitalist nondemocratic China offers not only a policy of non-interference but also a message of national particularism, international ideological pluralism, state sovereignty, strong state involvement, and indigenous cultural development. These are attractive not only to governments but also to peoples, as an alternative to American and Western dominance and as a counterforce to the sweeping blind forces of globalization.

A message need not be formulated in universalistic terms to have a broader appeal. Fascism during the 1920s and 30s was a very particularistic creed—it was nationalistic, based on "my country"— yet it had many devotees and imitators outside Italy, Germany, and Japan, who applied it to their own particular countries and societies. Compared to any other historical regime, the global liberal order is in many ways benign, welcoming, and based on mutual prosperity— so it is natural for people in the West to believe that everybody else would want to join it. And yet both Germany and Japan had to be literally pulverized before they were made to abandon some of their most cherished national traditions and join the liberal order. Likewise, a message might be deeply Chinese, deeply East Asian, and still be appealing to other societies that might reject the liberal model in search of something more native, more group-centered and os- tensibly more harmonious. China is in the process of opening a large number of Confucian cultural institutions around the world, which may share the success that other Asian spiritual systems have enjoyed in the West over the past decades. A fast-growing number of people are taking up the study of Chinese, above all in Southeast Asia, but also in other parts of the world, including, most fashionably, in New York private high schools.[17] The revival of China's rich cultural her- itage in movies, music, and other cultural forms could resonate as powerfully as India's Bollywood, through East and Southeast Asia, and beyond.

Does the greater power potential of capitalist authoritarianism mean that the transformation of the former communist great powers may ultimately prove to be a negative development for the democ- racies? It is too early to tell. Economically, the liberalization of the former communist countries has given the global economy a tremen- dous boost, and there is more in store. The possibility of a protec- tionist turn in the system must be assiduously avoided in order to prevent a grab for markets and raw materials. As we saw, such a grab followed the disastrous slide to imperial protectionism during the first part of the twentieth century, helped radicalize the capitalist nondemocratic great powers of the time, and precipitated both World Wars. Of course, the openness of the world economy does not depend exclusively on the democracies. In time, China itself might become more protectionist, as it grows wealthier, its labor costs rise, and its current competitive edge diminishes. As a huge market, it may choose to go on its own and/or in closed cooperation with its regional neighbors. We have seen such massive reversals in the past.

There are also other lasting benefits to the democracies from the transformation of the former communist powers. The collapse of the Soviet Union and the Soviet empire stripped Moscow of about half the resources it commanded during the Cold War, with Eastern Europe absorbed by a greatly expanded democratic Europe. This is one of the most significant changes in the global balance of power since the forced post-war democratic reorientation of Germany and Japan under U.S. tutelage.

If China does not eventually democratize and Russia does not reverse its drift away from liberalism and democracy, it will be critical that India remains democratic, given its potential role in balancing China if the latter adopts an aggressive posture, and the model it presents for other developing countries. But the most important factor remains the United States. For all the criticism leveled against it, the United States—and its alliance with Europe, Japan, and, indeed, India—stands as the main hope for the future of liberal democracy. Despite its problems and weaknesses, the United States still commands a global position of strength that it will likely retain even as the nondemocratic-capitalist powers continue their rapid growth. Not only does the U.S. have the highest GDP and productivity growth rate in the developed world; it also has greatest potential to grow further in population and hence in economic power. This is because the U.S. is an immigrant country, with only about one-fourth the population density of the European Union and China and one-tenth that of Japan and India. All these others are experiencing aging and ultimately shrinking populations.[18]

China's economic growth rate is the highest in the world and, given the country's huge population and still-low levels of development, such growth harbors the most radical potential for change in global power relations. But even if China's superior growth rate persists and its total GDP surpasses that of the United States by the 2020s, as is often forecast, China would still have just over one-third of the United States' wealth per capita, and, hence, considerably less economic and military power. Closing that far more challenging gap in high-technology with the developed world would take several more decades. Total GDP alone, without GDP per capita—as a measure of level of development—is a poor guide to a country's wealth and power. Invoking it to celebrate China's ascendancy as the world's third-, second-, or even largest economy, as is widely done, is highly misleading.[19] As it was during the twentieth century, the "United States factor" remains the greatest guarantee that liberal democracy, even if it cannot retain its present-day hegemony, will not be relegated to a vulnerable position on the periphery of the international system.

5

The Modern Transformation and the Democratic Peace

The idea that democratic or liberal states (there is some difference of emphasis here) never or very rarely go to war with each other is the most robust "law" discovered in the discipline of international relations.[1] This theory of democratic peace has great significance for the real world. In practical terms, it suggests that a world comprised of liberal/democratic states will be peaceful, an idea long championed by Thomas Paine, Immanuel Kant, and Woodrow Wilson. The theory has clear policy implications that drew the attention of President Bill Clinton's administration and became the centerpiece of President George W. Bush's foreign policy in the wake of the terrorist attacks on September 11, 2001.

I suggest that the democratic peace theorists have overlooked the defining development of the nineteenth and twentieth centuries that underlies that peace: the industrial-technological revolution. That revolution made democracy on a country scale possible, and, as previously described, also made all the countries that experienced the revolution—democratic and nondemocratic alike—far less belligerent than they had been in pre-industrial times. The inter-democratic peace represented only the most striking manifestation of that development. In reality, democracy is difficult to institute and sustain where economic and social modernization has not taken root; nor, before such development has occurred, would democracy alone necessarily lead to a democratic peace. This must be remembered in shaping policy towards undeveloped and developing countries.

The Evolution of a Theory

Introduced in the 1970s, the democratic peace theory has since gathered momentum and gained credence, withstanding extensive criticism and continuously being developed, amended, and refined in the process.[2] An agreement of sorts now prevails that during the nineteenth century, the democracy, liberalism, and democratic peace that existed only in the West were considerably weaker than they later became.

This is connected to another vexed issue raised in relation to the democratic peace theory: the role of popular pressure in starting wars. During the nineteenth century, as the masses moved to the forefront of politics and political systems underwent democratization, it was widely believed that militant popular pressure, rather than the wishes of reluctant governments, drove countries into war. Contrary to a prevailing view, popular agitation should not be attributed exclusively to leaders' manipulation of peace-loving peoples. Just as often, leaders were catering to a strong public demand. Particularly in liberal/democratic countries, the masses frequently swept cautious and peacefully-inclined leaders along with them. The word "jingoism" came into currency in late nineteenth-century Britain, at a time of increasing democratization, and denoted a chauvinistic and bellicose public frenzy. Jingoism was widespread during the Boer War (1899-1902). At the very same time (1898), waves of popular enthusiasm forced the American government's hand and carried the United States into war with Spain. Lest it be thought that the enemy in either of these cases failed to qualify as fully liberal/democratic, it should be noted that it was public opinion in both Britain and France that proved most bellicose, chauvinistic, and unsympathetic during the Fashoda Crisis (1898) between those two countries. It was the politicians who climbed down from war.

Moreover, the process of democratization has been said to promote war because it is closely associated with the assertion of hitherto suppressed ethnic identities and nationalist aspirations. Thus it has been claimed that although democracy ultimately decreases the likelihood of war, the initial process of democratization—the democratic transition—has the opposite effect.[3] Another formulation has it that partly-free states have been more war-prone than nondemocracies.[4] Historically, democratization and liberalization were processes that did not consist of a one-time transition from a nondemocratic regime but continuously unfolded, often over decades and even centuries. The asserted dichotomies of liberal/nonliberal or democratic/non-democratic, which long underlay the debate over the democratic peace, are crude and misleading.

Because liberal and democratic countries have become more so since the late eighteenth century, the inter-democratic peace was less secure in the nineteenth century West, and did not become entrenched until the twentieth century.[5] A number of major developments made early liberal/parliamentary societies progressively more liberal and democratic: the abolition of slavery; the gradual expansion of the franchise to all adult males and to females during the nineteenth and early twentieth centuries; the extension of equal legal and social rights to women and minorities; the rise in social tolerance in general; and the increase in political transparency and accountability during the second half of the twentieth century. As the standards of liberalism and democracy have continuously risen, the democratic peace has also deepened. It has been suggested that the frailness of peace between democracies in today's developing world can be explained by lower levels of democracy and liberalism compared to the developed West. In this respect, developing countries are reminiscent of the nineteenth-century West.[6]

The simplicity of the original democratic peace theory has been further compromised by the addition of other elements whose effects have been dynamic over time. Greater trade (relative to GNP) and greater trade openness (lower tariffs), advocated by liberals from Adam Smith and the Manchester School as a recipe for prosperity and peace, have been demonstrated to diminish the likelihood of war between countries.[7] Later studies have greatly expanded on the initial democratic peace concept with their findings that joint democracy, mutual and open trade, and joint membership in international organizations, each independently and significantly reduce war. They have thus endorsed all the original elements of Kant's "tripod for peace."*[8]

And yet Kant's logic (preceded by Paine's) is incomplete and somewhat flawed. A still broader perspective is needed to account for the liberal/democratic peace, to the extent that such peace has indeed been unfolding.

Liberalism, Democracy, Economic Development, and the Modern Transformation

What the democratic peace theorists have overlooked is the most profound transformation experienced by humanity during the nineteenth and twentieth centuries, or indeed ever: the industrial-technological revolution (see chapter 3). The effects of this staggering change have only recently begun to filter through into the discussion

* Erik Gartzke's claim that capitalist development alone, rather than democracy, is sufficient to explain the peace phenomenon is hard to rationalize. As his statistical analysis only covers the period after World War II, it leaves out the clash of the capitalist great powers in 1914. In addition, some (albeit weaker) interdemocratic peace existed even among highly protectionist democracies before 1945.

of the democratic peace. For example, it has been found that economically developed democracies are far more likely to be peaceful towards one another than are poor democracies. In fact, the democratic peace phenomenon between poor democracies has been found to be weak at best.[9] Economically developed democracies have also been far less prone than poorer democracies to fight civil wars.[10] Indeed, during the past couple of centuries, what has been on the rise and accounts for the growth of the democratic peace has been not only liberal countries' levels of democracy and liberalism, as democratic peace theorists believe, but also their wealth. Moreover, it should be emphasized that all these developments are not separate from one another but are closely intertwined. Democracy on a country scale and liberal societies emerged only in the nineteenth century and have evolved ever since not merely because they were suddenly recognized as good ideas, but rather because their growth was underpinned by the revolutionary changes taking place in the socioeconomic infrastructure during modernity.

As we have seen, though liberal democracies tend to be economically developed, development did not always go hand in hand with democracy. Nonetheless, poor democracies have been not only less war averse but also few in number and vulnerable to collapse and replacement by nondemocratic regimes.[11] True, economically developing, predominantly agrarian, stable liberal/democratic regimes existed in the nineteenth century. These included, most notably, the United States before the Civil War (though slavery still existed), and a growing number of European and Western countries. In the twentieth century, India is the most prominent member on this list. Yet not only were these cases few; in all of them, the industrial-technological revolution had already been brewing, and its products, such as the newspaper and the railway (and, in the twentieth century, the electronic media), were deeply affecting society and politics.[12] Furthermore, the more economically advanced a liberal/democratic society is the more liberal and democratic it becomes, with both these traits closely correlating with an aversion to war. During the 1990s, as democracy became the hegemonic model after the collapse of communism, some poor countries democratized. Yet comparative studies rank poorer democracies lower on the democratic and liberal scales, leading commentators to suggest the term "illiberal democracy" to describe some of them.[13] Some scholars hold that liberalism is more responsible for the democratic peace than is democracy. But both liberalism and democracy—and their interrelationship—have gained in strength in liberal/democratic countries experiencing economic development and greater wealth. Thus democratization and liberalization have been bound together with economic development and war aversion in the modern transformation.

This brings us to the puzzling question of how well the democratic peace theory applies to pre-modern times. If modern liberal/democratic states do not fight each other, should the same not hold true for earlier democracies, particularly those of classical antiquity? This question involves a special difficulty. The information that has survived from earlier times is painfully patchy even with respect to some of the best-documented cases, such as classical Athens and Rome. Knowledge about Greek city-states other than Athens (with the partial exception of Sparta) is extremely hazy. We possess nothing even remotely approaching a full record of their wars or their regimes, as we do with those of the nineteenth and twentieth centuries. Under these limitations, one comprehensive study has found that Greek democracies actually exhibited a somewhat greater propensity to fight one another than nondemocracies or mixed dyads did. The most dramatic case involved the famous Athenian campaign against Syracuse (415-413 BC) during the Peloponnesian War.[14]

Another study argues that ancient republics, too, never fought each other.[15] Yet a few examples will suffice to falsify this claim. Many of the known democracies of ancient Greece belonged to the Athenian Empire of the fifth century BC. The empire was coercive and oppressive, with Athens compelling city-states to join and preventing them from leaving by means of its overwhelming force. Rebellions were harshly put down. Athens also prevented members of the alliance from fighting one another. After Athenian power had been severely weakened during the later stage of the Peloponnesian War, the allies, including democratic ones, rebelled in great number. Thus ancient Greece's record during the fifth century BC mostly represents democratic imperial coercion rather than inter-democratic peace.[16]

The fourth century BC offers an even more significant test, partly because the number of Greek democracies had increased. When a second Athenian-led alliance was formed in 377 BC, it was based on voluntary and egalitarian principles. To weaken Sparta, Athens assisted in restoring independence in Thebes. Not only did Thebes become a democracy; it reestablished the Boeotian League on a democratic basis. In 371 BC, the Boeotian army under the generalship of Epaminondas smashed the invincible Spartans in the Battle of Leuctra. A dramatic change in the Greek balance of power followed. Spartan hegemony and tyrannical imperial rule were broken, while Thebes rose to prominence. Invading the Peloponnese, Epaminondas assisted Sparta's satellites in breaking away and forming democracies and regional democratic leagues. He also freed a large part of Sparta's enslaved subject population, the helots. And yet these noble acts, obviously advantageous to Thebes, were vigorously opposed by none other than democratic Athens. After Leuctra, it was Theban hegemony, rather than Spartan, that Athens feared and balanced against.

In 369 BC, Athens joined the war against Thebes, allying itself against Greek freedom with oligarchic and oppressive Sparta and its oligarchic allies, Greek tyrants such as Dionysius of Syracuse and the blood-thirsty Alexander of Pherae, and foreign, autocratic Persia. For seven years, the two great Greek democracies were engaged in a war that raged all along their imperial peripheries. The war involved numerous encounters, culminating in the Athenian participation against Thebes in the Battle of Mantinea (362 BC). It was the greatest battle in Greek history until then, in which Epaminondas again won a crushing victory but was killed. Theban hegemony and the war thereby came to an end. As Athens attempted to reassert its own hegemony, its conduct towards its allies began to resemble its first empire, prompting a rebellion known as the Social War (357-355 BC) that broke the power of the alliance. Lest Thebes' conduct towards other democracies be considered saintly, remember that Thebes conquered and razed to the ground its old rival, democratic Plataea (373 BC).

Surprisingly, the record of republican Rome's wars in the Italian peninsula has not been examined at all in this context and appears to be no less questionable with respect to the democratic peace phenomenon. Classical scholars continue to debate how democratic the Roman Republic was, with recent trends swinging in the more democratic direction.[17] Ancient historian Polybius, in his book *The Histories* (VI.11-18), classified Rome as a mixed regime, in which the people's assemblies and tribunes, the aristocratic senate, and elected officials balanced each other's power. It should be noted, however, that our own modern liberal democracies, too, would probably have been classified as mixed regimes by the ancients, and unlike ancient republics, they do not include popular assemblies of all citizenry that directly legislate and decide on issues such as war and peace. Knowledge about the internal regimes of the other Italian city-states is meager. Still, to argue that none of the hundreds of Italic and Greek city-states in Italy that were brought under Roman rule were republics—that Rome was in fact the only republic in Italy—is untenable. For example, Capua and Tarentum, the two leading city-states of southern Italy that defected from Rome during the Second Punic War and were harshly crushed by it, were both democratic republics at the time (Livy, XXIII.ii-vii, XXIV.xiii). Indeed, Polybius (VI.5), following Aristotle (*The Politics*, II.11 and IV.8-9), judged Carthage, Rome's rival during the Second Punic War, to be a mixed regime polity, in which the populace (which supported the Barkaide war party) dominated more than it did in the Roman Republic itself.[18] Not only did this democratic character not prevent the war; but neither in these nor in any other case does the evidence with respect to public deliberations in Rome on war and peace include even a reference to the enemy's regime as an issue meriting consideration.

Those who emphasize liberalism above democracy as the explanation for the modern phenomenon have claimed that classical democracies can hardly be considered liberal, since they practiced slavery and in general did not uphold the liberal rights and other republican preconditions required by Kant, such as a separation of powers (Rome's mixed regime notwithstanding).[19] However, this interpretation is not fully satisfactory either because slavery existed in the United States until the Civil War, long after the proponents of the liberal/democratic peace theory count the U.S. as a liberal and democratic state. As already mentioned, other liberal democratic traits were also still relatively weak or absent in many of the countries listed as liberal/democratic by the democratic peace theorists. On the other hand, whereas Athens has become proverbial for the perils of direct democracy, in the Roman Republic, for example, institutional constraints were very strong. A popular assembly of the people in arms, the *comitia centuriata*, was called to vote for war, but only after the senate debated and decided on war and a motion for war was introduced in the assembly by a consul (or, theoretically, a praetor) who was elected annually in highly competitive elections.

Paine and Kant subscribed to the Enlightenment view that selfish autocrats were responsible for war. According to that view, if the people were given the choice, they would recoil from war because they carried the burden of war and incurred its costs. But it was the populace in Athens, not the aristocrats, that pushed for aggressive imperial expansion and war, even though the people fought in the army, manned the rowing benches of the Athenian navy, and had to endure war's destruction and misery, as in the forced evacuation of Attica during the Peloponnesian War. Rome's military prowess and tenacity similarly derived specifically from its republican regime, which successfully co-opted the populace for the purpose of war. Historically, democracies proved particularly tenacious in war precisely because they were socially and politically inclusive. And again, in pre-modern times, they did not refrain from fighting each other.

Why, then, did the citizens of Athens and Rome, for example, repeatedly vote for war? Why did they endure devastating and protracted wars for years and years, including, as we have seen, against other democracies/republics? It was not because they were less democratic than modern societies, but because in the agrarian age in which they lived, war could provide great material benefits. First, there was booty to be had. Furthermore, in Athens, the empire levied lavish tributes that financed about half of the Athenian budget, paying for the extensive public construction and huge navy, in both of which the people were employed (Plutarch, *Pericles*, 12). Moreover, the empire's might boosted Athenian trade supremacy, which, in turn, increased its resources and enhanced its might. Finally, poor Athenians were allocated farms in colonies (*cleruchies*) established on territory confiscated from defeated enemies. Although Rome did not levy tribute from its satellite "allies," it confiscated an enormous amount of land from those it defeated throughout Italy and established on it colonies of Roman citizens and Rome's closest allies, the Latins.

This was the logic of war in pre-industrial times. Some change may be discernable with the commercial city-state republics of Renaissance Italy, though whether because of republicanism or commercialism is not clear.[20] However, as seen in chapter 3, the decisive shift took place with modernity, steeply rising wealth, and commercial interdependence. It has been argued that the Kantian "tripod for peace" transformed the vicious circle of anarchy, mutual insecurity, and war into a virtuous circle of peace and cooperation.[21] But it was in fact industrialization and the escape from the Malthusian vicious circle that underlay the tripod.

The striking fact that proponents of the democratic peace overlook is that nondemocratic countries, too, fought much less during the industrial age than they had in earlier times. In line with what we saw in chapter 3, in the century after 1815, nondemocratic/nonliberal great powers such as Prussia and Austria (which were not colonial powers) engaged in war far less frequently than Britain and France and dramatically less than in their own earlier histories: once every eight or nine years, compared to once every two years (Austria) or three years (Prussia) during the eighteenth century that more or less represented the European great powers' average during early modernity. Furthermore, the nondemocratic and nonliberal great powers shared the general sharp decline in the frequency of great-powers wars, to about one-third of their rate in early modernity.[22] During the twentieth century this trend encompassed the communist as well as the capitalist great powers, and, indeed, augurs well for today's capitalist nondemocratic China and Russia.

The reasons why the democratic peace theorists overlooked this overall sharp decline in the occurrence of war are natural enough: liberal and democratic countries emerged only during the past two centuries, so it seemed reasonable to focus only on these centuries. In addition, the most extensive and widely used database of wars, the Correlates of War, only covers the period from 1815 on. As a result, few have compared that period to the pre-1815 era. Nor have the democratic peace theorists asked why liberal and democratic societies only started to appear during the past 200 years or so, and how this fact is related to the defining development of that period: the onset of the industrial-technological age. The whole question of democratic peace has been considered outside its defining historical context.

Still, it is true that liberal and democratic societies have exhibited greater war aversion than nondemocracies during the industrial age, as mainly demonstrated in their relations with each other. Why is this so? A number of related reasons have been at work. In some nonliberal and nondemocratic industrial countries, a militant ethos, often associated with a traditional warrior elite, was deeply embedded in the national culture. Both Germany and Japan were led from above to national unification and modernization and came late to the imperial race. They had relied in the past, and expected to rely in the future, on military force to assert their claims. Statism had been and remained central to their modern development. Conjointly, they either rejected the logic of free trade in the name of national economy and/or feared that the global liberal trade system would give way to closed imperial blocs, leaving them out in the cold. In communist countries, the total rejection of the market principle went hand in hand with their ideological commitment to its destruction by force. Furthermore, nonliberal and nondemocratic countries that were repressive at home were little inhibited from practicing repression abroad. Contrary to a widely held view, it has been shown that their empires could and did pay off.[23]

Liberal democratic countries have differed in crucial respects. Socialized to peaceful, law-mediated relations at home, their citizens have come to wish and expect the same norms to be applied internationally. Living in increasingly tolerant, less conformist, and argumentative societies, they have grown more receptive to the Other's point of view. Liberal democratic powers initially possessed the largest colonial empires; but as they increasingly promoted freedom, legal equality, and (expanding) political participation at home, they have found it more and more difficult to justify rule over foreign people without their consent and/or without granting them full citizen and voting rights. At the same time, liberal democracies that sanctify life, liberty, and human rights have ultimately proven to be failures in forceful repression (see chapter 7). Liberal economy, dominant despite periodic lapses, rejected war and military subjugation in favor of peaceful economic growth and mutually-beneficial trade. Furthermore, with the individual's life and pursuit of happiness elevated above group values, the sacrifice, let alone self-sacrifice, of life in war has increasingly lost legitimacy in liberal democratic societies. Democratic leaders have shared these values or been forced by public pressure to conform to them—or have been removed from office. As scholars tend to agree, "normative" and "structural" factors are intertwined in creating the democratic peace.

For these reasons, although nonliberal and nondemocratic states also became much less belligerent in the industrial age, liberal democracies have been the most attuned to its pacifying aspects. This applies most strikingly to the democracies' relations among themselves, but, as scholars have become increasingly aware, also to their conduct in general. Initially, it was widely believed that liberal/democratic states were peaceful only towards one another, because they fought nondemocratic states and appeared to be as prone as those states to initiate wars. However, further analysis has suggested that liberal/democratic countries in fact fought fewer interstate wars than did nondemocracies, although they were involved in more "extra-systemic" wars, mainly colonial, against non-state rivals.[24] Because of their far-flung colonial empires and consequent "colonial wars," old liberal and democratic powers such as France and Britain fought far more often than nonliberal great powers such as Austria and Prussia-Germany. However, although this finding is statistically true, statistics can be misleading if they are not properly contextualized. Having acquired their empires when colonial victories were still winnable on the cheap, liberal democracies were stuck with them as the democracies became increasingly inhibited from engaging in forceful suppression. Insurgencies thus flared up into full-scale and protracted colonial wars, whereas nondemocratic powers either lost their empires in the World Wars or suppressed insurgencies so effectively that they did not explode into wars (see chapter 7).

Moreover, when the number of casualties incurred is taken into account—rather than just looking at wars and war years—the evidence shows that during the twentieth century, liberal democracies have suffered far less, or put differently, have engaged in wars that were far less severe. The severity of wars, not just their frequency, should be considered in measuring war avoidance.[25] In part, the liberal democracies suffered fewer casualties because of an accidental reason: they were only briefly involved in major ground warfare during the highly lethal World War II, having been disastrously defeated in 1940 in western Europe, from which they were thrown out until June 1944. Other than that, they also suffered fewer casualties in their wars because they tended to possess technological superiority over rivals from the world's undeveloped areas. Wars with weak rivals are far less severe for the more advanced power, and hence are more easily entered into than full-scale interstate wars.[26]

Finally, during the twentieth century, advanced liberal democracies' constitutional and consensual nature shielded them from civil wars, historically the bloodiest type of war and one that tended to plague old-style autocracies and oligarchies, as well as weak democracies (consider the American and Russian civil wars, nineteenth-century Europe in general, and today's developing world). And although totalitarian regimes, too, avoided civil wars by means of ruthless repression, many of them killed their own citizens in horrific numbers as a matter of course.[27] Thus it has been argued that liberal democracies kill their own people far less than other regimes do.[28]

Other Contributing Factors

Additional factors associated with the modern transformation may be involved in making affluent liberal democratic societies more averse to war. It is common among social scientists to regard parsimony as an ideal and to dislike "laundry lists" of causes. Yet, without quarreling with the theoretical proposition, a multiplicity of factors is at play in social phenomena, often making theoretically less elegant explanations truer. Some of the additional factors suggested below are variably related to liberal democracy, while others are associated with economic development, which, in turn, is also variably related to liberal democracy.

Wealth and Comfort—Again. Throughout history, rising prosperity has been associated with a decreasing willingness to endure the hardship of war. Freedom from manual labor and luxurious living conditions achieved by the rich in prosperous premodern societies conflicted with the physical strain of campaigning and life in the field, which became more alien and unappealing. As the industrial-technological age unfolded and wealth per capita rose exponentially, the wealth, comfort, and other amenities once enjoyed only by the privileged elite spread throughout society. Thus increasing wealth has worked to decrease war not only through the modern logic of expanding manufacturing and trading interdependence, but also through the traditional logic of the effect of affluence and comfort on society's willingness to endure hardship. Because new heights of affluence and comfort have been achieved in the developed world in the post-World War II era, when nearly all the world's affluent countries have been democracies, it is hard to distinguish the effects of comfort from those of democracy in diminishing belligerency.

It is difficult for people in today's liberal, affluent, and secure societies to imagine how hard life was for their forefathers only a few generations ago, and how hard it remains today in poor countries.

Angst may have replaced fear and physical pain in modern societies; yet, without depreciating the merits of traditional society or ignoring the stresses and problems of modernity, this change has been nothing short of revolutionary. People in pre-modern societies struggled to survive in the most elementary sense. The overwhelming majority of them went through a lifetime of hard physical labor and a constant struggle to escape hunger. The tragedy of orphanage, of child mortality, of premature death of spouses, and of early death in general was an inseparable part of their lives. People of all ages were afflicted with illness, disability, and physical pain, for which no effective remedies existed. Even where state rule prevailed, violent conflict between neighbors was a regular occurrence and an ever-present possibility, putting a premium on physical strength, toughness, honor, and a reputation for all of these. Misery and tragedy tended to harden people and make them fatalistic. In this context, the suffering and death associated with war were endured as just another natural affliction, along with Malthus's other grim reapers: famine and disease.

Life changed dramatically with the emergence of affluent liberal societies. In addition to the decline of physical labor, hunger and want were replaced by abundance, and food became available practically without limit. In fact, food became so available that obesity rather than starvation is a major problem, even—and sometimes especially—among the poor. Infant mortality fell to about one twentieth of its rate during pre-industrial times. Annual general mortality declined from about 30 to about 7-10 per 1,000 people.[29] Infectious disease, the number one killer of the past, was rendered virtually nonlethal by improved hygiene, vaccinations, and antibiotics. Countless bodily irritations and disabilities—deteriorating eyesight, bad teeth, skin disease, hernias—that had been an integral part of life, were alleviated with medication, medical instruments, and surgery. Anesthetics and other drugs, from painkillers to performance enhancers, dramatically improved the quality of life.

Today, people in the developed world live in well-heated and air-conditioned dwellings equipped with mechanical-electrical appliances. They have indoor bathrooms and lavatories. They wash daily and change clothes as often. They drive rather than walk. They are flooded with popular entertainment to occupy their spare time. They take vacations in far-away, exotic places. They embrace "post-modern," "post-materialistic" values that emphasize individual self-fulfillment. In an orderly and comfortable society, rough conduct in social dealings decreases, while civility, peaceful argument, and humor become the norm. Men are more able to "connect to their feminine side." Whereas children and youth used to be physically disciplined by their parents and fought among themselves at school, on the playground, and in the street, they are now surrounded by a general social abhorrence of violence. Social expectations and psychological sensitivity have also risen dramatically. People in affluent liberal societies expect to control and enjoy their lives, rather than merely enduring them, and war scarcely fits into their plans.

It is not surprising, then, that the "imprudent vehemence" historically associated with republican foreign policy greatly diminished in the affluent, consumer-hedonistic, liberal democratic societies that developed after World War II. Indeed, this change has had more impact on the elites and affluent middle class than on the less affluent population.

Metropolitan Service Society. The growth of city and metropolitan life is a somewhat related phenomenon. Commercial and metropolitan cities were considered by classical military authorities, such as Vegetius, echoed by Machiavelli, as the least desirable recruiting ground, particularly compared to the countryside with its sturdy farmers accustomed to hard physical labor. The residents of large metropolitan centers typically immigrated from diverse quarters and lacked the traditional communal bonds of solidarity and the social controls of village and small-town communities. Exposed to the cities' quick dealings and temptations, they were regarded as too fickle, rootless, undisciplined, and cynical to be trusted. With modernity, urbanism in large metropolises steadily expanded to encompass the majority of the people. Correspondingly, the number of people living in the country declined. Yet the military continued to regard them as the best "recruiting material."

Examples abound. With the coming of the twentieth century, the German army drafted disproportionately from the countryside, and its second choice was country-town people. It limited recruitment in the large cities, where the masses were regarded as militarily less suitable and, infected with socialism, as politically suspect.[30] Liberal democratic Britain, the world's most urban society, adopted the draft in both World Wars. There, too, country folk were regarded as best fit for military service. Industrial workers were considered less desirable, and office workers were deemed the least suitable for the rigors of military life. Notably, the British Empire's best troops during both World Wars came from the farms of the still predominantly rural dominions: New Zealand, Australia, and Canada. Similarly, the farmer recruits from Middle America who dominated the United States' armies during World War I were regarded as first-class military material. The American armies of World War II, which included a larger number of city dwellers, still fought well enough, but did not enjoy the same superb reputation as had their World War I predecessors. And Vietnam War draftees, especially those from urban states, had an even worse reputation for natural soldierly qualities. An analysis of the hometowns of the fallen in the Iraq War reveals that rural and small-town communities contribute nearly twice as many volunteer-recruits per population as do metropolitan centers.[31] Israel's crack military units during the first decades of its existence were overwhelmingly comprised of young people from a relatively small number of voluntary communal villages (*kibbutzim*) and farm communities (*moshavim*).

One factor that must be considered is the far-reaching change in the occupations within society and especially the cities during this period. City-folk during the zenith of the industrial age were mainly factory workers. They were accustomed to physical labor, machines, and the massive, coordinated work regime labeled "Fordism" and "Taylorism." They lived in dense urban communities and were mostly literate. These qualities were major strengths for the military, especially as the military, too, was undergoing mechanization. However, as the industrial-technological era progressed, manufacturing declined and the services sector expanded its share of the workforce in the most advanced economies. In the United States, which led this trend, 70 percent of the workforce is now employed in services while only 18 percent work in manufacturing.[32] It can be argued that the military, too, has been moving from mechanized to information-based forces, increasingly relying on computerized data processing and accurate fire from afar to do most of the fighting. All the same, adaptation to military life comes far less naturally to people from contemporary affluent societies who are accustomed to deskwork in the office and the seclusion of residential suburbia than it did to their farmhand and factory-worker predecessors. Again, while high rates of industrial urbanism characterized not only liberal societies but also Imperial and Nazi Germany and the Soviet Union, nearly all the advanced service economies are associated with liberal democracies, making the effect of the two factors hard to distinguish.

The Sexual Revolution. Sexual promiscuity is another factor that may have dampened enthusiasm for war in advanced modern societies, especially among unmarried young men. Young single males who traditionally constituted the most aggressive element in society, now find a variety of outlets for their restlessness. Joining the military for foreign adventure, which once lured many of them away from dull and suffocating countryside and small-town communities, has lost much of its attraction, especially for city-dwellers, who can find excitement and adventure close to home. At the same time, state military authorities have curtailed the sexual aspects of military service.

In modern imperial Japan, the troops still indulged in state-tolerated mass rape while serving abroad, some of it in the form of state-organized, forced prostitution. At least two million women are estimated to have been raped by Soviet soldiers in conquered eastern Germany in 1945. Mass rape was a major feature of the ethnic wars in Bosnia and Rwanda during the 1990s, as it continues to be in Darfur and West Africa. In the armies of the Western democracies, although rape is severely punished, American and other Allied troops widely availed themselves of an abundant supply of low-cost prostitution in ruined Western Europe after World War II and, later, in desperately-poor Vietnam.[33]

All in all, however, the increased sexual opportunity in society radically changed the incentives to enlist for war. Young men now are more reluctant to leave behind the pleasures of life for the rigors and chastity of the field. "Make love, not war" was the slogan of the powerful anti-war youth campaign of the 1960s, which not accidentally coincided with a far-reaching liberalization of sexual norms. Again, this liberalization mainly took place in affluent and urban liberal societies, though it is interesting to speculate how much it affected the Soviet Union in later periods and how it may affect today's China. There is no need to fully accept the reasoning of Sigmund Freud, Wilhelm Reich, and Michel Foucault to appreciate the significance of this factor.

Fewer Young Males. In addition to changes in the circumstance and attitudes of young males, the significant decline in their relative number is another factor that may have diminished enthusiasm for war in contemporary developed societies.[34] In premodern societies, life expectancy not only at birth but also for adults was considerably lower than it is today. Thus the share of young adult males in the adult population was higher. With the onset of industrialization, as child mortality fell sharply and birthrates followed only slowly, the number of young adults in a fast-growing population increased not only in absolute terms but also relative to the total adult population. This was evident in the nineteenth-century West, as it was in the twentieth-century developing world. Young male adults were most conspicuous in the public enthusiasm for war in July–August 1914, as they were in all wars and revolutions. In today's affluent societies, however, with birthrates falling below replacement levels and with increased longevity, young adults—including males—constitute a shrinking portion of an aging population. Before World War I, males aged 15 to 29 constituted 35 percent of the adult male population in Britain, and 40 percent in Germany; by 2000, their share had dropped to 24 percent and 29 percent, respectively. By comparison, young adult males of the same age cohorts constituted 48 percent of Iran's population in 2000.[35]

Some scholars have suggested that because young males have always been the most aggressive element in society, while older men were traditionally associated with a counsel of moderation and compromise, the decline in young men's relative number may contribute to the growing war aversion of developed societies and explain the greater belligerence of developing ones, particularly in the Muslim world. China's "one child" policy may make it more similar to a developed society; but in Islamic societies, booming population growth peaked only recently, and the relative share of young men is at its height.[36] Avoiding simplistic correlations, the restlessness of the cohorts of young adult males in Islam should be understood in conjunction with the lack of economic (and sexual) opportunity in traditional, stagnant, and culturally defensive societies. At the height of the population growth in industrially booming Britain, around the middle of the nineteenth century, the share of young adult males was over 40 percent of the adult male population, not unlike the proportion in Iran today, and yet this was the period of the *pax Britannica*.

Fewer Children per Family? Given the sharp decline in birthrates in developed societies, Edward Luttwak has suggested that the far smaller number of children per family may be the cause of these societies' decreased belligerency. According to this argument, when a typical present-day family only numbers one to two children, it is much more agonizing for parents to lose a child.[37] This reasoning, however, hardly stands up to scrutiny. Historically, only the period of demographic explosion during early industrialization saw families with many surviving children. Although birthrates had indeed been much higher in pre-modern societies, infant mortality was also higher, resulting in an overall demographic equilibrium. Women gave birth to many children, but only a few survived to adulthood, keeping average numbers at about the replacement rate. Thus, having raised their few surviving children to adulthood, parents in the past could no more easily "afford" to lose them than can today's parents. Economically, parents then could less afford to lose their only support in old age. Certainly, mortality and other calamities were a more normal part of life in the past, to which people necessarily resigned themselves. Furthermore, in traditional societies people were simply helpless to oppose the dictates of far-away and alien authorities, who did not care about their wishes, or, indeed, about their life and death. Where the people themselves ruled, as in city-state republics, the expected rewards of war—offensive and defensive—made the risks to life more acceptable. Both conditions have lost much of their validity in advanced modern liberal democracies.

Women's Franchise. While young men have always been the most aggressive element in society, men in general have always been more aggressive and belligerent than women. Having won the right to vote in twentieth-century liberal democracies, women have been able to influence governments' policies by electing the government. Studies in the West in recent decades have shown a consistent gender gap in attitudes toward the use of military force.[38] Such differences might play a significant role in tilting the electoral balance against military ventures in modern affluent liberal democracies. Women's voting record has been suggested as one of the factors that accounts for why liberal democracies became more averse to war in the twentieth century than they had been in the nineteenth.[39]

It should be noted, though, that women are not unconditionally pacifist. In some societies and conflicts, the attitudes of the sexes do not diverge significantly. For example, no such divergence has been evinced in studies of both sides of the Arab-Israeli conflict. The authors of these studies have suggested that their findings are most likely explained by the high "salience" of the conflict, which generates high mobilization levels among members of both sexes.[40] Similarly, in the 2004 American presidential elections, the so-called "security moms," who feared additional mega-terror attacks at home, cast more votes for the ostensibly tougher candidate, George W. Bush, than they did for his Democratic challenger. In Russia, mothers' voices that had been mute in the totalitarian system during the Soviets' failed Afghan campaign (1979-1988), became dominant during the first Chechnyan war (1994-1996), after Russia had become liberalized. Mothers took to the streets in public demonstrations, significantly contributing to the Russian decision to withdraw. However, the continuation of Chechen terror attacks on Russian soil after the Russian withdrawal legitimized Russian re-intervention in the eyes of Russian public opinion, which encompassed men and women alike.

Nuclear Weapons. The advent of nuclear weapons is widely regarded as the crucial factor that has prevented a great-power war since 1945. However, as noted previously, the "long peace" since 1945, the longest yet in the modern great power system, was preceded by the second and third longest peaces ever between the Western powers in the years 1871-1914 and 1815-1854. Crucially, of course, nuclear weapons have all but prevented the interruption of such extended periods of peace with devastating interstate wars such as those that had occurred before 1945. This is a monumental change. And yet something had been changing in the relations between industrializing/industrial great powers, and particularly between industrial liberal democratic great powers, long before the arrival of the bomb.

The advent of nuclear weapons marks a turning point in history. Yet the resulting restraint is based on arms races, deterrence, and the balance of terror, and leaves room for covert, indirect, and low-intensity forms of armed conflict. At the same time, however, any sort of violent conflict between modern affluent liberal democracies has become virtually unthinkable, irrespective of the bomb. A "positive" rather than "negative" peace prevails among them.

All the above elements are interconnected in the modern transformation, each with its own contributing effect coming into play at different points in time, reinforcing the war aversion of the societies involved. Some readers may find my argument problematic, because the effect of each of the above variables is difficult to isolate, let alone measure. To achieve such isolation, variation among the relevant cases is needed, yet it does not always exist. Affluent societies only emerged after World War II and all have been liberal democracies. Had nondemocratic and capitalist Germany and Japan survived World War II and become affluent, the effect of prosperity could have been tested more effectively. If China becomes affluent while remaining nondemocratic, such a test may yet turn out to be feasible. The same applies to the metropolitan service society, and largely also to the sexual revolution, with the very limited test-cases offered by the later Soviet Union and today's China. The complexity of the causal web is demonstrated by the number of young males during the *pax Britannica*, which is similar to the number in today's Islamic world. Women's voting may be quite significant, though it is difficult to isolate. Indeed, a true generalized, theoretical understanding of reality can only be achieved if it incorporates the relevant range of causal factors.

Conclusion: Past and Future

The industrial-technological revolution has been transforming the world over the past two centuries. It is in the context of this radical transformation that the democratic peace theory must be understood to be basically true, though in need of amendment. A far more complex causal process has been at work than a simple relationship between an independent variable, liberal democracy, and a dependent one, democratic peace.

The emergence of the democratic peace phenomenon sometime during the nineteenth century has been linked, without further questioning, to the evolution of liberal/democratic regimes. But, indeed, that evolution was made possible by the modern transformation: the growth of "imagined communities" of print; a commercial-industrial economy; "mass," urban, society; mass literacy; the bourgeois way of life; and growing commercial wealth. The democratic peace phenomenon has been intimately connected with these underlying processes and has increased with them. It did not exist among premodern democratic and republican city-states, not because they were not democratic or even liberal enough politically, but because they were not yet modern. This is the piece of the puzzle missing from the visionary tracts of Paine and Kant, if only because they themselves predated most of that transformation.

The modern transformation accounts for the fact that not only liberal democratic countries but all countries, once swept into the industrial-technological age, engaged in war far less often than they previously had, a fact overlooked by the democratic peace theorists. This being acknowledged, the liberal democratic countries' path to modernity has involved a distinctly greater aversion to war than that of nondemocratic and nonliberal countries for the political, economic, social, and normative reasons specified above. These manifest themselves most strikingly when both sides to a potential conflict are liberal and democratic.

Other factors that flow from the modern transformation apply mostly to liberal democratic countries, while being only variably connected to their regime type. These include the staggering rise in standards of living; the decrease in hardship, pain, and death; the dominance of metropolitan life and the service economy; the spread of the consumer and entertainment society; the increase in sexual promiscuity; the enfranchisement of women; and the shrinking percentage of young males in populations.

How does this reframing of the democratic peace thesis affect current policy questions? There are implications for the capitalist nondemocratic great powers, and above all China. The more modern and affluent China becomes, the stronger the pacific trends within it are likely to become, even if China does not democratize. However, this projection should be qualified in several ways. First, much depends on the global economy's remaining open and not retreating into state and regional protectionism. Second, militancy could increase during the process of China's modernization and in the period of transition, because of strong domestic nationalism and instability and the change in the global balance of power as hegemonic power relations shift. Third, China may become more rather than less militant as it grows in strength and assumes the role of a superpower. Fourth, affluent liberal democracies' relations with a nondemocratic China are unlikely to be as thoroughly pacific as relations among themselves.

A hotter current debate concerns whether the United States and its democratic allies should adopt an active and even forceful policy of promoting democratization. The debate has focused mainly on the developing parts of the world. After the collapse of the communist challenge, and as the democratic peace theory took hold in the 1990s, the Wilsonian notion that the United States should actively pursue democratization as a means of creating not only a just but also a peaceful world gained widespread currency, becoming official policy in the wake of 9/11. Yet although there is much validity to the theory, it has tended to ignore some crucial impediments and lent itself to simplistic interpretations.

In the first place, as President Wilson and his successors discovered in failed efforts to establish democracy through intervention—including military intervention—in Mexico, the Dominican Republic, Haiti, Nicaragua, Costa Rica, and Guatemala, democracy is neither desired by all nor unconditionally sustainable. Furthermore, the adoption of democracy is not merely an act of will but has tended to occur on a country scale in conjunction with economic and social modernization. As Wilson himself came to appreciate: "The real cause of the trouble in Mexico was not political but economic." Elections would not address "the prime cause of all political difficulties," which was the highly unequal pattern of land distribution and, hence, of social relations. Consequently, the president grew skeptical about the ability of foreign intervention to generate real change.[41]

The forceful democratization of Germany and Japan after World War II, the most successful such cases in the twentieth century, were possible not only because of the political circumstances of defeat in total war and the communist threat, but also because each possessed a modern economic and social infrastructure upon which a functioning liberal democracy could be built (though it required overcoming considerable cultural resistance to democracy and liberalism in both countries).[42] Efforts to bring democracy to countries that lack both a liberal tradition and a modern socio-economic infrastructure—countries that are largely tribal and fraught with ethnic and religious cleavages—should persist, but their limitations must be recognized. Democratization will be a gradual process, and it can backfire under excessive pressure, threatening stability in moderately pluralistic state-societies, where the main opposition is not liberal and democratic but Islamist, and often undemocratic and radical. Not only the public discussion but also much of the scholarly work seems to have lost sight of the fact that even the United States, Britain, and France became liberal and parliamentary decades, if not centuries, before they became democratic. In fact, before modernization, the elites in all these countries feared that if the people were given the vote, they would not choose liberalism or democracy, let alone moderation and peace. Indeed, in France, for example, such popular tendencies were demonstrated in the wake of both the Great Revolution and the 1848 Revolution.

Second, the democratic peace phenomenon tends to be much weaker in the early stages of liberalization, democratization, and economic development. Thus it is not at all clear that the democratization of Arab and Muslim states would by itself reduce the militancy of their societies. As in nineteenth-century Europe, and contrary to the prevailing cliché, public opinion in Arab and some non-Arab Muslim states tends to be more militant than that of the semi-autocratic state rulers, who struggle to keep such popular pressures in check. The semi-democratic Islamic regime in Iran that replaced the autocratic Shah in a popular revolution has been highly militant, no different in this respect from revolutionary France's republican regime. Although religious authorities in Iran must approve presidential candidates and disqualify those whose Islamic credentials are suspect, it is still the case that the more fundamentalist and militant candidate Mahmoud Ahmadinejad won a sweeping victory over the less extreme Akbar Hashemi Rafsanjani in the 2005 popular elections. Popular support for Iran's nuclear program transcends social and political divides. In the first democratic Algerian national elections ever, held in December 1991, the radical Islamic Salvation

Front won, prompting an intervention by the army to prevent an Islamic regime and leading to murderous civil war.

A similar scenario unfolded in the Palestinian territories, where the militant Islamic movement Hamas won the 2006 elections, resulting in a bloody clash with Fatah, the movement that had dominated the Palestinian Liberation Organization (PLO) for decades. The Hamas takeover of Gaza followed, as did a heightened conflict with Israel. Only the presence of the Israeli army prevents similar occurrences in the West Bank. Hamas is more popular there than the more pragmatic Fatah-led Palestinian Authority, whose peace negotiations with Israel enjoy little support. In Egypt and Jordan, the peace treaties their rulers signed with Israel are unpopular, most notably with the middle classes and the intellectuals, the ostensible agents of democratization and pacification. The independent and highly popular satellite network Al Jazeera, broadcasting from Qatar, is hailed as a major catalyst of democratization in the Arab Middle East because it undermines autocratic state rule. While this is true, it should be noted that the network's message is distinctively nationalist and sympathetic towards militant groups. In Lebanon, the more democratic the political system becomes through the incorporation of the largest ethnic community, the Shia, the more the country is dominated by the militant Shia organization, Hezbullah, and the more it finds itself in conflict with Israel. Indeed, the resulting 2006 war arguably contradicts the doctrine of inter-democratic peace. How ethnically divided Iraq will develop under its American-sponsored democratic regime has yet to be seen.

Of course, Arab and Muslim countries do not constitute a monolith, and should democratization occur within any of them, the consequences in each may be different. Democratization, which is often advanced as a remedy for such societies, should be understood as part of a more complex causal web, in which economic and social modernization are necessary (yet by no means sufficient) for success-ful democratization and liberalization, all of which together effect democratic peace.

6
The Democracies' Way in Conflict

If affluent modern liberal democracies are indeed more war-averse than nondemocracies, does this pacificity also manifest itself in conduct during wartime—that is, *in bello* as well as *ad bellum*? This question has attracted far less scholarly attention than the democratic peace proposition. During World War II, the liberal democracies showed few scruples in wreaking total destruction from the air on Germany and Japan, exceptionally brutal enemies with which they were locked in a life or death struggle. Apprehension about the liberal democracies' supposed "crusading spirit" was also expressed during the early stages of the Cold War and in the wake of 9/11, echoing David Hume's charge that popular governments exhibit "imprudent vehemence" in conflict situations. Nevertheless, it is argued here that the liberal democracies demonstrate far greater restraint in conflict situations than do nondemocracies.

One noted aspect of liberal democracies' restraint is their tendency to eschew preventive war.[1] Historically, they have chosen not to initiate war even when they were threatened, held the military advantage, and were in danger of losing it. The British reluctance to seriously consider "Copenhagening" the German navy during the massive German naval buildup prior to World War I is a case in point. The term alludes to Lord Nelson's preemptive destruction of the Danish navy in 1801 to prevent it from joining Napoleon.

More strikingly, the liberal democracies did not intervene by force in the mid-1930s to prevent Hitler's Germany from rearming, even though it meant they would lose the complete military superiority they held over Germany. Hume would cite this decision as evidence of his other charge against liberal countries: that they tend to show "careless and supine . . . complaisance" towards the future.[2] On the other hand, a war not initiated may be a war averted, and there is no way of determining this in advance.

The United States demonstrated the same conduct against the Soviet challenge after World War II. It is generally forgotten that between 1945 and 1949, the United States possessed a monopoly over nuclear weapons. Theoretically, it had every reason to preempt without fear of retaliation rather than to adopt a strategy of containment and wait for Soviet nuclearization, which, although expected to come later than it actually did, was acknowledged as inevitable.[3] Theories of nuclear restraint often overlook this fact. Had it been the Soviet Union or Nazi Germany, rather than the United States, that possessed a nuclear monopoly, there can be little doubt that either would have pressed for the massive production of nuclear weapons and carried out a world-wide policy of conquest and coercion. Thus not only with other affluent liberal democracies but also with its Soviet archrival, the United States refrained from pressing its overwhelming advantage to the point of war.

The liberal democracies' strong inhibitions against preventive war would be challenged and would become the focus of a bitter public controversy in connection with the American "war on terror" after September 11, 2001. But recoiling from preventive war comprises merely one element of liberal democracies' typical conflict behavior.

The Attitude Shift and the Search for Alternatives to War

The notion that serious war is an unmitigated disaster and constitutes sheer madness increasingly took hold in the newly formed liberal democratic countries at the outset of the twentieth century, as the global industrial, trading, and financial system expanded and interdependence deepened. Norman Angell's famous book, *The Great Illusion* (1910), posited that it was an illusion that any side could gain from a modern major great-power war, restating the traditional liberal rationale that had increasingly materialized. It was against this background that World War I caused such a crisis in the liberal consciousness and traumatized liberal societies. Political scientist John Mueller has asserted that the trauma was a historical turning point that affected all powers alike, curing modern society of the predilection for war.[4] But this was not the case. The decline in belligerency did not start with World War I. On the contrary, the war came in the wake of the relatively peaceful nineteenth century, after by far the longest and second-longest periods of peace in European history. Nor was the deep trauma that developed in the aftermath of the war the result of the great losses of life and treasure in themselves. Again (as Mueller recognizes), these were not greater, relative to population and wealth, than the losses suffered in massive wars throughout history. The novelty was that liberal opinion now regarded such wars as wholly out of step with the modern world. The famous "trauma" of the war was a liberal phenomenon, closely correlated with the strength of liberalism in each country rather than with that country's actual losses.

Britain, for example, was Europe's most liberal power, and the retrospective reaction against the war and the mourning for the "lost generation" were the greatest there, even though Britain's losses were the smallest among European powers. British casualties—three-fourths of a million dead—were terrible, but amounted to no more than 12 percent of British troops enlisted during the war. They were smaller in absolute terms, and even more so relative to population, than France's loss of almost 1½ million and Germany's 2 million dead. And yet the reaction against the war in Germany was far more limited than that in Britain.[5] Only liberal (and socialist) opinion, which was less dominant in Germany than in Britain, responded negatively. The most famous anti-war author was Erich Maria Remarque, a German liberal and pacifist. Certainly there was much war weariness and a widespread loss of enthusiasm for war in Germany, which, relative to its population, had suffered twice as many casualties as Britain. But Germany also had strong nationalist, anti-liberal, right-wing elements that vehemently opposed those anti-war sentiments. Ernst Juenger's books, glorifying his experience in the trenches and exalting the qualities of war, competed with Remarque's for popularity in Germany. Similarly, powerful nostalgic evocation of soldierly trench camaraderie played a major role in turning formerly liberal democratic Italy in a fascist direction.

Perhaps the two cases that best illustrate the correlation between the post-World-War-I trauma and the level of liberalism are the United States and Serbia. The mightiest power in the world was not afflicted by heavy losses and crippling economic costs, as were the European belligerents. The United States suffered relatively light casualties in its brief involvement in the war and gained tremendously from the war materially, replacing Britain as the world's leading banker, creditor, and insurer. Nonetheless, it was in the United States that the onset of disgust with the war and regret over participating in it was the most rapid and sweeping. By comparison, the small and backward Serbia suffered, relative to population, the heaviest casualties of all the warring nations and was totally ravaged by the war and occupation. Nevertheless, Serbia hardly experienced the trauma of, and disillusionment with, the war. Nor, indeed, would other traditional societies that suffered hundreds of thousands and millions of casualties in the wars of the twentieth century (up to and including the Iran-Iraq War and Iraq's later gulf wars) react more traumatically than had been the norm among pre-industrial societies. By contrast, as the twentieth century ran its course, the smallest number of casualties has become sufficient to discredit a war in affluent liberal societies, particularly when the threat is not considered existential, imminent, or unsusceptible to alternatives to war, or when the prospects of achieving victory seem dim.*

Most people in post-World War I Britain probably would not have denied that the stakes in that war were high and that it would have mattered if Britain had lost the war to Germany. Yet, they felt (even if they were not always able to articulate precisely) that the war had conflicted with the economic and normative rationale of the modern world; that everybody had more to gain from peace, and everybody had lost from the war, even if some had lost more than others. It was the powers' slide into, and persistence in, the war, given the alternatives, that was regarded as disastrous and sheer madness.

Given the liberal democracies' fundamental attitude, the problem of how to deal with conflict has become a torment for them. Initially, liberals, while peacefully inclined, were not pacifist, because

---

* **Note on casualty sensitivity:** Eric Larson, *Casualties and Consensus: The Historical Role of Casualties in Domestic Support of US Military Operations* (Santa Monica, Calif.: Rand, 1996); C. Gelpi, P. Feaver, and J. Reifler, "Success Matters: Casualty Sensitivity and the War in Iraq," *International Security*, 30:3 (2005/2006): 7-46; and Gelpi, Feaver and Reifler, "How Many Casualties Will Americans Tolerate?" *Foreign Affairs*, 85.1 (2006), have claimed that American casualty sensitivity is overrated. They demonstrate that it was actually a function of the public's assessment of the prospects of achieving military victory. However, nondemocratic and less-developed countries are less susceptible to this constraint, and their casualty tolerance in general is much higher. Moreover, liberal democracies' very ability to achieve victory in some types of war has been severely constrained by their self-imposed norms (see chapter 7), which takes us back to square one: liberal democracies are more casualty-sensitive because they are liberal and democratic.

liberty had to be won and defended, even if by force. In time, some liberals (and socialists) came to espouse more or less unilateral pacifism. This, however, lacked a convincing explanation of what to do if the other side is not similarly pacifist, and so never became a dominant creed. More in tune with the liberal mainstream has been the effort to make the entire international system conform to the Painean-Kantian-Wilsonian model—that is, to have it embrace democratic self-determination, liberalism, and free trade, link into the modern spiral of mutual prosperity, and resolve disputes through international institutions. Where the conditions for that model materialized, as they did most notably in post-World War II Western Europe, the results were truly remarkable. But most of the world proved highly resistant to that model, and much of it still is.

Where a Painean-Kantian peaceful accommodation fails to materialize, because not all states are liberal (and affluent), there remains Saint-Pierre's idea of collective security, whereby all states combine against those that disturb the peace. This idea was central to the League of Nations and to the United Nations, but by and large it has failed for reasons long ago sensed by Rousseau: powerful states and coalitions cannot easily be restrained by the threat of overwhelming collective action; the threat remains mostly theoretical, because states exhibit scant willingness to get involved in a conflict not their own; in the absence of a coercive authority that would prevent free-riding, states expect others that are more closely involved to do the job; states often have a greater interest in maintaining good relations with the aggressor; and determining who the aggressor is involves value judgments, about which no consensus can be reached. All this applies to democratic as well as to nondemocratic countries. The revived pleas in the post-Cold War era, and especially after 9/11, for collective security by consent through the United Nations greatly underestimate all these problems.[6]

Isolation, Appeasement, Containment and Cold War, Limited War

As long as the world has not become fully affluent, liberal, and democratic, and collective security remains largely ineffective, liberal democracies have been obliged to cope with the prospect of conflict and war. Their strategic policy in facing this prospect has typically followed a pattern, progressing on an upward scale from isolationism to appeasement, containment and Cold War, limited war, and only most reluctantly, to full-fledged war. As with other aspects of the liberal democracies' distinctive behavior, this pattern began to manifest itself during the latter part of the nineteenth century and crystallized in the twentieth.

Where isolationism could be adopted, it has been a most tempting option for liberal democracies. However, in a shrinking world of growing interdependence, it has become increasingly untenable. Furthermore, even where no significant interests are involved, the liberal commitment to universal values and human rights often makes a foreign disturbance hard to ignore.

When faced with a significant threat that could not be shut out, the liberal democracies' option of second resort has been to compromise with a rival by accommodating some of its demands and offering it economic rewards. This option is cheaper than war, rests on the affluent liberal democracies' strongest asset—their abundant resources—and holds the prospect of integrating the rival into a mutually beneficial economic relationship that may eventually also lead to its liberalization. The success of such a policy of appeasement hinges on whether the other side chooses to accept the deal and become a partner, or views the offer as a sign of weakness that only whets its appetite. Thus states must appease from a position of strength and must dangle sticks in addition to carrots.

If appeasement fails, containment and Cold War are the next steps in the sequence. These involve building a deterring coalition, applying economic pressure, and engaging in covert subversion and ideological warfare. Finally, if an armed conflict breaks out, liberal democracies attempt to limit its scope. They most often do this by providing money and hardware to cement coalitions and strengthen local forces against adversaries; employing blockades and naval and aerial actions, in which developed countries possess a clear superiority; and staging limited operations by technologically superior strike forces. Direct large-scale warfare, especially on land, where casualties might be high, has become the least desirable option. All these, of course, are "ideal types" that often overlap. If they sound as if they come from today's headlines, their application in fact is of long standing.

During most of the nineteenth century, both Britain and the United States adopted isolationist policies. Britain was the first to be drawn out, when an external threat—most notably Germany's double challenge to Europe's continental balance of power and to Britain's naval supremacy—could no longer be contained without foreign commitments. Even then, however, Britain repeatedly sought in vain a combined naval, colonial, political, and economic deal that would bring about a *rapprochement* with Germany. And when war came, British policy was predicated on the assumption that most of the land war would be shouldered by France and Russia. Britain initially intended to confine its contribution primarily to the naval, amphibious, and economic spheres, with the blockade serving as its principal weapon. Only the imminent danger of its allies' collapse eventually forced Britain into full-scale military participation.[7]

The United States, for its part, was able to maintain its isolation for much longer. And even when he formally took his country to war in April 1917, President Wilson did not plan full-scale involvement in the European carnage. The United States, too, was forced into full participation only by the near collapse of France and Italy and the specter of British defeat in the U-boat campaign in the summer of 1917, the collapse and defection of Russia by the turn of the year, and the imminent disaster on the Western Front in spring 1918.

By the mid-1920s, the Western democracies' elites increasingly felt, in the spirit of John Maynard Keynes's *The Economic Consequences of the Peace* (1920), that the punitive Versailles treaty had been a mistake. During the "Locarno era" they attempted to reach accommodation with Germany by helping it to revive its economy, by normalizing its international status, by integrating it into international institutions, and by holding before it the prospect of further peaceful settlement of its grievances. Unfortunately, this attempt collapsed with the post-1929 world economic crisis. During the 1930s, the actions of Japan, Germany, and Italy against the international status quo posed acute threats to the liberal democracies. Nonetheless, in all the liberal great powers—the United States, Britain, and France—the public's mood and the consensus in the political parties and the government were unmistakably against war, even when the democracies still held the military advantage. Again, their policies evolved from isolationism to appeasement, to containment and Cold War, to limited action. Total war was imposed on them by their enemies. All the liberal great powers trod that road.[8]

Isolationism was the preferred option of those who felt they could embrace it successfully: the British toyed with the idea and then adopted a policy of partial isolationism in the form of "Limited Liability," which ruled out the commitment of substantial ground forces to continental Europe; the United States espoused isolationism more fully and for a longer period of time. However, given the magnitude of the threats, isolationism in itself was deemed to be insufficient. Both countries augmented the policy with efforts to ease the conflict and tame the Axis powers, especially Germany, by addressing some of their grievances and offering them economic rewards and beneficial trade deals. Most vigorously pursued by Neville Chamberlain, appeasement failed because ultimately Hitler's ambitions surpassed anything the liberal democracies were willing to accept. It should be noted, though, that those of Chamberlain's peers who opposed his policy did not object to appeasement as such, but believed it had to be more circumspect and buttressed by force.

During the Ethiopian and Spanish crises, the Western democracies still had little appetite for action in what they perceived as too small a threat. All the same, consider the type of strategies that were suggested (though mostly not implemented) counter to the Axis moves. Rather than direct military intervention, they included economic sanctions, the isolation of both Ethiopia and Spain by the Allies' vastly superior naval power, and the supply of armaments to the Ethiopians and to the Spanish Republicans. In any event, it was only the Czechoslovak crisis in the spring of 1938 that greatly alarmed Western opinion. The strategic ideas pressed in opposition to appeasement again fit the pattern. In Britain, Anthony Eden, David Lloyd George, Winston Churchill, the British Labour and Liberal parties, and in the U.S., President Franklin Roosevelt, all held that Germany had to be contained by a superior coalition (incorporating the Soviet Union), capable of deterring Germany or, failing that, of strangling it economically.

Roosevelt's line of thought with respect both to Europe and the Far East was typical. In late 1937, following Japan's invasion of China and the signing of the Anti-Comintern Pact among Germany, Italy, and Japan, the president increasingly aired the notion of a coordinated policy of sanctions and containment against the aggressors. The idea was embodied in his famous "quarantine speech" of December 5, 1937. Later, during the Czechoslovak crisis, Roosevelt called for a "siege" of Germany. He suggested that the European Allies close their borders with Germany, even without declaring war, and stand on the defense, relying on the economic blockade to do the job. The United States would back them economically.[9]

By the time war came in 1939, Germany had become less susceptible to economic pressure because of its domination of south-
eastern Europe and its pact with the Soviet Union. Under these
circumstances, the "twilight" or "phony" war being waged on the
Western Front was not a curious aberration, as it is customarily regarded, but the most natural strategy for Britain and France. Having
lost their ability to contain Germany within its old frontiers, choke
it economically if it attempted to break out of them, or militarily
defeat it and recover Eastern Europe from its grip, Britain and
France in effect opted for more or less the same strategic policy that
the West would adopt against the Soviet Union after World War
II. They relied on armed co-existence, containment, economic pressure, and ideological and propaganda warfare. Militarily, Britain and
France restricted themselves to peripheral and indirect action, trying
to avoid escalation to full-fledged war. In all but name, this was a
policy of containment and Cold War. They hoped that over time,
as the Western bloc formed its defenses and deployed its resources,
the Germans would be forced to seek an accommodation with the
West. They also hoped that the Nazi regime might mellow or lose
power. Unfortunately, the whole concept collapsed in May-June
1940, when Germany succeeded in decisively defeating the Allies
and overran Western Europe.

The United States followed a similar path. In 1940-1941,
American policy in both Europe and the Far East encompassed all
means short of open war. A crucial element in Britain's decision to
keep fighting in the summer of 1940 was Churchill's belief that the
United States would enter the war before long, probably after the
presidential election in November. This did not happen. Massive
American economic aid in the form of Lend-Lease enabled Britain
to continue the fight. But the prospect of an American declaration
of war remained a dubious matter throughout 1941. During the summer of that year, the United States extended Lend-Lease to the So-

viet Union, took over the battle against the German submarines in the western half of the Atlantic, and garrisoned Iceland. Nevertheless, it became clear to the British that American entry into the war was not to be expected in the near future. The majority of Americans and members of Congress objected to the war, and Roosevelt's own intentions were unclear. He was surely not going to allow Britain to fall, and probably would have used the United States' growing weight to steadily increase American influence on the course of the war. But was he waiting for more progress to be made on U.S. rearmament, and using the time to prepare American public opinion for eventual participation in the war? Or was he quite satisfied with the existing situation, wherein Britain and the Soviet Union carried the burden of fighting, with massive American political and economic support but without full American participation? These questions remain in dispute and will probably never be answered conclusively. It is doubtful that Roosevelt himself knew. It was only Japan's surprise attack and the subsequent German declaration of war on the United States that decided the issue. Neither Britain nor the United States embarked on all-out war until forced into doing so by the surprising collapse of their defenses, in May-June 1940 in Western Europe, and in December 1941 in the Pacific, respectively.

Although far more powerful than Japan in all respects, the United States deployed non-military means to contain Japan in 1940-1941. Washington tightened economic sanctions so strongly that the imposition of an oil embargo threatened to bring Japan to its knees. Unfortunately, defensive precautions to back up this policy proved insufficient. As it had with Germany the year before, the policy of containment, economic coercion, and Cold War floundered when the enemy did the unthinkable, and in a highly successful lightening campaign, broke down the walls that had been built up against it.

By the end of World War II, the Soviet Union was taking the place of the Axis powers as the liberal democracies' major potential rival. And, yet again, the democracies' response followed a path leading from appeasement to containment and Cold War. As revisionist historians of the 1930s have reminded us, towards the end of the war, Roosevelt and Churchill recognized Soviet control over Eastern Europe for much the same reasons that Chamberlain had been prepared to see German hegemony extended over that region. Roosevelt in particular hoped to come to terms with the Soviet Union and incorporate it within a new global four-power collective security system. By 1946-1947, however, American hopes were dashed, and the policy of containment and the Cold War came into being.

As noted above, this policy was adopted when the United States still held the monopoly over nuclear power. All the same, according to George Kennan, the intellectual architect of containment, the idea was formed in a fundamentally non-nuclear frame of mind and derived from pre-1945 experiences.[10] The atomic bomb is not even mentioned in either his "Long Telegram" from Moscow in February 1946 or his famous "Mr. X" article in *Foreign Affairs* in 1947—containment's formative documents. Throughout the second half of the 1940s, Kennan insisted that the United States must refrain from using nuclear weapons as an active instrument of diplomacy and war. Periods of heightened tensions and greater militarization alternated with periods of *rapprochement* and *détente* until the end of the Cold War.

In the nuclear age, the prospect of a major great-power war diminished, and it appears to have become even more remote since the collapse of the Soviet Union and the communist challenge. Yet, if conflict with the capitalist nondemocratic great powers were to develop, the liberal democracies' typical pattern of conduct would likely replay itself, because it is deeply rooted in the democracies' fundamental condition and outlook.

With the exception of the preventive war in Iraq, carried out in the special circumstances of the "war on terror" (see chapter 8), the same pattern has manifested itself even in liberal democracies' conflicts with far smaller and weaker, economically backward, non-democratic rivals. Most typically, the pattern has been unfolding in the effort to stop and reverse the nuclearization of North Korea; and the full range of options—from appeasement, to containment, Cold War, and limited war—is being practiced or entertained by the U.S. and its democratic allies vis-à-vis Iran, to keep it from crossing the nuclear threshold. The preventive strike option causes the greatest controversy, even though Iran is no great-power rival, as the Soviet Union was between 1945 and 1949, and nuclear weapons would make it immune to military action, give it a much freer hand in one of the world's most sensitive and vital regions, and possibly create runaway nuclear proliferation among the region's other powers. If a policy of appeasement and economic coercion fails, some in Washington advocate containment of a nuclear Iran as the main alternative to a preventive war. It remains to be seen how this dilemma unfolds.

This pattern of conflict behavior has had a mixed and often disappointing record since it began to crystallize in the early twentieth century. The methods involved are politically and strategically difficult to apply, often ineffective, and carry their own psychological strains. Still, given the nature of modern liberal societies, this way of making war appears to be the norm.

7
Why Counterinsurgency Fails*

Counterinsurgency has become such a problem for the liberal democracies' way of warfare that it deserves a special chapter. Down to the present Iraqi and Afghan entanglements, insurgency warfare has earned a reputation for near invincibility, driving the democracies out of their former colonial empires during the twentieth century and frustrating military interventions even where the asymmetry in regular force capability is the starkest. Why have mighty powers that proved capable of crushing the strongest of opponents failed to defeat the humblest of military rivals in some of the world's poorest and weakest regions?

It is argued here that, rather than being universal, this difficulty has overwhelmingly been the lot of liberal democratic powers—and has been encountered precisely because they are liberal democratic.[1] While it may seem obvious, this proposition is still far from being generally recognized by scholars and in the public discussion at large.[2] The crushing of an insurgency necessitates ruthless pressure on the civilian population, which liberal democracies have found increasingly unpalatable. Premodern powers rarely had a problem with such measures, nor have modern authoritarian and totalitarian powers been reluctant to use them—and overall they have proved quite

* This chapter was written with Dr. Gil Merom of the University of Sydney.

successful in suppression. Indeed, suppression was the sine qua non of their imperial rule. Like the other distinctive traits already described, weakness in counterinsurgency is peculiar to the liberal democracies' conflict behavior.

The Secret of Suppression and the Liberal State

Throughout history, imperial pacification rested on the overt threat and actual application of ruthless violence to crush resistance in subject societies. Where the people offered insurgents support and sympathy, they were exposed to sweeping reprisals by the ruling power, including killing, looting, burning, and enslavement. The *ultima ratio* of imperial control was the threat of genocide. All empires worked this way, including democratic and republican ones, such as ancient Athens and Rome. They could only work this way.

During the Peloponnesian War, the Athenians reneged on their earlier decision to kill all the men and enslave the women and children in conquered Mytilene, which had defected from their empire (428 BC). Instead, they opted for the execution of "only" some 1,000 men held responsible for the rebellion, which, given the size of the polis, still amounted to a very large part of its male population. The Athenian leader Cleon was nonetheless dismayed by this show of leniency,[3] but his expressed fear that democracies were incapable of ruling others turned out to be unsubstantiated (or at least premature), as the Athenians' famous dialogue with, and ultimate annihilation of, the people of Melos (416 BC) chillingly demonstrates. Republican Rome's record in dealing with insurgents was even more merciless.

However, the conduct that had sustained empires throughout history became increasingly unacceptable in the emergent liberal societies of the modern era. As with other elements of the liberal/democratic peace, this was a gradual and uneven process.

Some mellowing of practices towards civilian populations was already discernable in Western Europe during the Age of Enlightenment. Yet in Europe's more backward areas, and with respect to non-whites, practices remained very much as before. Despite sporadic British atrocities, the rebelling American colonists benefited from this mellowing, intermixed as it was with the Royalist desire not to further alienate the colonial population.[4] But the people of Ireland—that "Africa in Europe" for the British—rebelling in 1798, still bore the brunt of the British suppression that had broken their backs in blood and fire in earlier uprisings in previous centuries, and had crushed forever the rebellious "savage" Scottish Highlanders after the Battle of Culloden (1746). The Americans' treatment of the indigenous peoples during the nineteenth century (though the great majority of them fell victim to European diseases; see chapter 8) was similarly legitimized by their perception of them as savages. The French "pacification" of Algeria and Indochina during that century still relied on the old methods. Notably, however, Marshal Bugeaud's methods in Algeria were denounced by a delegation of the Chamber of Deputies, headed by Alexis de Tocqueville, which recommended the adoption of a "Continental standard of conduct."[5] The bloody Indian Mutiny (1857) was the last that the British Empire suppressed atrociously, in the old ways, though in this case, too, it should be noted that the troops' retributions lacked official sanction.

The establishment of Britain's Liberal Party in 1859 marks a symbolic turning point in British attitudes. That this had a significant impact on various aspects of British international conduct can be seen in the British attitude towards the Russian-supported rebellion of the Bulgarians against their Ottoman masters (1875-1878). It had been Britain's policy to back the Ottoman Empire against any Russian advance towards the Mediterranean, but the British public's outrage at the Turkish atrocities in suppressing the Bulgarian rebel-

lion—the mass killings, torture, and rape—fueled by journalistic re-
ports and by William Gladstone's missionary agitation, tied the
British government's hands. The Ottoman Empire was defeated by
Russia and forced to give up the rebellious province. "Foreigners
don't know what to make of the movement; and I am not surprised,"
Foreign Secretary Lord Derby told Prime Minister Benjamin Dis-
raeli. A German observer noted that it would be almost inconceiv-
able in any Continental country.[6] No longer was British policy
conducted on purely "realist" considerations of power. In mid- and
late-Victorian Britain, human rights became inseparable from the
public debate on foreign policy.

Soon enough, the same attitude arose with regard to Britain's
own empire, first in its white parts but later everywhere. The same
Gladstone, as a Liberal prime minister, opened the process that
would lead the Irish within a generation to an independent state, after
the liberal recipe for self-determination within the United Kingdom
failed to satisfy them. How did a country that had been under the
British heel for centuries suddenly succeed in seceding? The rise of
modern nationalism in Ireland cannot be the only explanation, because national movements were successfully curbed and crushed by
ruthless nonliberal powers. It was only when liberals could no longer
resist the demand for self-determination, as well as finding the old
methods of forceful suppression repugnant and unacceptable, that
Ireland was able to gain independence. Needless to say, the process
was anything but smooth. The Liberal Party was split over the Irish
question and lost power for two decades. The Easter Uprising in
Dublin in 1916 was put down by robust force, and a full-scale insurgency took place between 1919 and 1921, when Britain decided to
pull out. Although British counterinsurgency tactics had proved quite
effective, they could never completely quell the rebellion, given the
restriction on ruthlessness towards civilians under which British
forces operated.

Nor was Ireland an isolated case for Britain. In the Boer War in South Africa (1899-1902), Britain initially suffered humiliating defeats in regular fighting at the hand of the forces of the Free Orange and Transvaal Republics. When a half-million British troops were dispatched to South Africa, the course of the war was reversed and regular Boer resistance was crushed, only to give way to widespread irregular resistance. Unable to subdue that resistance, the British resorted to draconian measures, rounding up the Boer civilian population into concentration camps. Some 30,000 people perished in the camps from various illnesses. And yet Britain was able to declare victory only by offering the Boers the most generous of peace terms, which within a few years effectively surrendered to them government powers over all of the South African Federation. South Africa and Ireland were signs of things to come in liberal democracies' counterinsurgency wars.

Alternative Explanations and Queries

Since the American humiliation in Vietnam, several explanations have been advanced to account for the puzzle of the weak defeating the strong. For one, it has been suggested that the problem lies in the number of troops and resources the strong country can spare for a particular local war, given its overall commitments and the difficulties of power projection to faraway theaters.[7] Most recently, the American problems in pacifying Iraq after its occupation in 2003 have been widely attributed to the commitment of too small a force (as if the deepening and failed American commitment in Vietnam had never taken place). Admittedly, security conditions have considerably improved following the American troop reinforcement during the "surge"; but without a far-reaching indigenous change, most notably in the attitude of Sunni tribal leaders, the surge would have yielded little fruit. Massive force commitment and considerable military success ultimately failed to keep France in Algeria and Israel in densely-populated Palestinian territories (or in Lebanon, where Israel achieved lesser military success). This was so even though in both cases the campaigns were perceived in their respective countries as their main theaters of operation and of vital national significance.

The Algerian and Israeli cases, as well as Ireland's, largely pull the carpet out from under another explanation for the puzzle: that developed powers' limited investment and much lower breaking points represent a lower interest and, hence, lesser motivation in the conflict than those of the indigenous force, a factor that ultimately decides the outcome. The argument suggests that the "balance of resolve" has outweighed the "balance of capabilities" in such unequal wars.[8] Most irregular conflicts have taken place in the undeveloped and developing parts of the world, whether in a colonial or post-colonial setting. Liberal economists have always stressed that maintaining colonies did not pay, and, in any case, the countries in question were and remain among the world's poor. As a result, this argument goes, the developed powers' interest in them was low, and once the costs of staying mounted, the incentive to pull out became irresistible. It should be noted, however, that Ireland was not a far-away colony but had been an integral part of Britain for centuries. Algeria, too, was regarded by the French as part of metropolitan France. The possibility of retreat tore France apart and brought it to the brink of civil war, not least because it involved the uprooting and removal of European settlers who had lived in Algeria for generations. The same applies even more to Israel and the territories occupied in 1967, which constitute the core of the country historically and geographically. And in Iraq, of course, the stakes are higher than anywhere else in the developing world, because of the implications of a withdrawal not only for the "war on terror" but also for the stability and security of a region that contains the world's richest oil reserves.

Moreover, the notion that effective counterinsurgency is costly obscures the issue that is at the heart of the matter: effective curbing of resistance can be achieved on the cheap if a country is willing to adopt indiscriminately ruthless measures, such as those that have been employed as a matter of course historically and by contemporary authoritarian and totalitarian countries, but that liberal democracies find repugnant. Counterinsurgency warfare becomes expensive and ineffective only when alternatives to ruthlessness are sought.

The awakening of modern nationalism is widely perceived as a crucial factor in galvanizing indigenous resistance. However, although there is some validity to this argument, it fails to explain the much greater success of nonliberal powers in subduing others, including— as we shall see—societies in which nationalism was fully developed.

The liberal democracies' record of failure in counterinsurgency warfare is frequently attributed to the effects of television coverage. It should be noted, however, that Britain lost the struggle against Irish independence long before television, as was effectively the case with the loss of its empire in general. Similarly, the French lost their war in Vietnam before the advent of television that would later allegedly lose the war for the Americans in the same theater. Even the French defeat in Algeria (1954-1962) effectively predated the age of television coverage. American television coverage of the war in Vietnam became negative only at a late stage, when it became clear that the United States had little hope of winning.[9] Television's transmission of the horrors and atrocities of war, like the effect of earlier mass media—the newspaper, radio, and newsreel—only reinforced a trend that was already strongly in evidence and was becoming ever-stronger as liberal sensibilities deepened.

The image of near invincibility that insurgency, guerrilla, "asymmetrical" warfare has acquired stands in stark contrast to its often low military effectiveness. Insurgents have rarely been able to defeat regular armies militarily, and they sustain far greater losses than they inflict, sometimes crippling losses. Nor is it accurate that modern affluent liberal democratic countries tend to lose wars against irregulars because of the democracies' inability to withstand protracted wars of attrition and their need to decide a war rapidly, as some scholars have claimed.[10] In both World Wars, grinding attrition was actually the democracies' strategy of choice, whereas their rivals, Germany and Japan, sought rapid decision by lightening campaigns. In the Cold War, too, it was the liberal democracies that outlasted the Soviets in the protracted conflict of materiel and endurance. Indeed, eight years of war for the French in Algeria and eight for the Americans in Vietnam hardly constitute short struggles. Conversely, the brutality of authoritarian regimes often cuts insurgencies short, so that in most cases the authoritarian stamina need not be put to the test. Liberal democracies have tended to lose protracted irregular wars against far less developed societies because their self-imposed restrictions on violence against civilian populations have ultimately rendered their often-successful military operations futile. Only when a significant (liberal) portion of their publics realized that no decisive, war-ending victory was possible under these circumstances did they turn against the continuation of these wars. Unable to win, they turned to withdrawal as the default option.

This is not to say that the balance of interests has nothing to do with the outcome. It is important to note that on the rare occasions when insurgents' demands go beyond withdrawal from their native territory, the balance changes. Irish resistance dislodged Britain from most of Ireland but has not been able to achieve a similar result in the predominantly Protestant parts. Palestinian resistance drove Israel out of most of the West Bank and the whole of Gaza, but when Palestinian suicide bombing intensified in Israel in pursuit of more far-reaching Palestinian goals, Israel successfully reoccupied the West Bank. Forced out of southern Lebanon by Hezbullah in 2000, Israel surprised Hezbullah in 2006 with the magnitude of its (mishandled) response to that organization's further encroachments. And in December 2008-January 2009, Israel inflicted a similar surprise on Hamas, which had been launching rockets from Gaza into Israeli towns. The Chechens drove Russia out during its liberal phase in the 1990s, but severe terrorism by Chechen extremists in pursuit of further demands led to a Russian reoccupation. Liberal democracies may find it very difficult to win even when pushed to the wall; but in such circumstances they, too, are capable of enduring a conflict and outlasting the insurgents by not losing. Although insurgents are often able to force far stronger liberal powers to withdraw from insurgents' home territories, they are unable to force capitulation.

A study of interstate wars in the period since 1815 claims that democracies have been at least as inclined as nondemocracies to target civilians, if not more so. The British starvation blockade of Germany in World War I and Allied city bombing campaigns against Germany and Japan in World War II are major examples. But indeed, as the same study emphasizes, such instances predominantly occurred in desperate major wars for survival—a category that excludes the overwhelming majority of counterinsurgency wars against weak nonstate rivals. Furthermore, the study documents (though barely takes into account) a change in the overall trend after 1945, which greatly intensified during a period of growing liberalism after 1970, in which democracies have targeted civilians less than nondemocracies have in interstate wars. The study's conclusions are open to dispute on various grounds.[11] All the same, among other things, it may suggest that the more intense the threat, the more likely are liberal democracies to relax their restrictions on the targeting of civilians in counterinsurgency operations as well.

Critics may remain unconvinced that self-limitations have really affected liberal democracies' conduct, and argue that during the twentieth century they still wielded formidable instruments of coercion and pressure in counterinsurgency wars and were often quite brutal. Atrocities, tacitly sanctioned by political and military authorities, or carried out unauthorized by the troops, have regularly been committed against both combatants and non-combatants. All the same, strict restrictions on the use of violence against civilians constitute the legal and normative standard for liberal democracies. And although many, probably most, violations of this standard remain unreported, numerous incidents have been exposed in open societies with free media, and are met with public condemnation and judicial procedures. Indeed, the effect of liberal public opinion and the media has been mightily reinforced over the past decades by the courts' increasing involvement in the policy process through judicial review, which in the opinion of some has made "lawfare" almost as decisive as warfare. All these developments radically limit the liberal democracies' powers of suppression, judged by historical and comparative standards. The fact that not only a massacre such as that of My Lai during the Vietnam War but also the terror and intimidation practices at Abu Ghraib prison in Iraq evoke the most resounding outcry is an illustration of the continuous rise in the standards of conduct that liberal democracies apply to themselves.

Skeptics might also question the notion that ruthless brutality is the *sine qua non* of successful counterinsurgency suppression, on the grounds that it conflicts with the "winning of hearts and minds" that has been posited as the key to success in the current liberal democratic discourse. Indisputably, winning over at least the elites of conquered societies—through benefits, cooptation, and the amenities of soft power—has always played a central role in imperial "pacification," as Tacitus (*Agricola*, 21) memorably described with respect to the taming of the barbarian Britons by Rome. Yet that velvet glove always covered the iron fist that had crushed local resistance mercilessly in the first place, and remained unmistakably in place as the *ultima ratio* of foreign control. To be sure, winning hearts and minds continues to be an important component in successful counterinsurgency; but it has become the liberal democracies' indispensable guideline for the pacification of foreign societies only because they have practically lost the ability to crush such societies by force if the latter choose to resist. This problem is scarcely felt by nonliberal democratic powers.

The use of urban environments by insurgents is a striking demonstration of the point. Traditionally, insurgency flourished mostly in the remote parts of the countryside. Urban environment constitutes a deadly trap against an enemy who has no scruples about indiscriminately felling buildings and setting cities on fire, as in the past, or razing them to the ground from a safe distance with artillery fire, as in modern time, with little regard for the inhabitants. This traditional rationale was demonstrated by President Hafez al-Assad of Syria, who in 1982 had whole neighborhoods in the city of Hama destroyed with artillery fire as his army brutally suppressed a revolt by the Muslim Brotherhood, killing an estimated ten thousand to twenty-five thousand of the city's population in the process. The Muslim Brotherhood was crushed so severely that it remained ineffective for nearly 20 years, throughout the presidency of the elder Assad. The Russian conduct in Grozny has been similarly ruthless, leaving large parts of the city in ruins but practically eliminating Chechen resistance there.

By contrast, irregulars fighting against liberal democratic powers make the cities their bastions precisely because they are able to blend into and take shelter within the urban-civilian environment, while relying on their opponents to refrain from operating indiscriminately in these settings. Thus the devastation caused by Israel in the villages of southern Lebanon, from which Hezbullah fired rockets on Israeli towns and villages during the 2006 Lebanon war, created an outcry both in Israel and abroad. This was so even though Israel had issued warnings to the inhabitants to leave, and "only" about 1,000 Lebanese were killed—many, perhaps the majority, members of Hezbullah. The reaction replayed itself during the Israeli operation in Gaza in 2008-2009, which Israel had been hesitant to carry out, despite the rockets routinely fired on Israeli civilians, precisely because of Gaza's dense urban population among which Hamas interwove itself in order to gain cover. In Iraq, too, the cities of the Sunni triangle and Baghdad proved to be the greatest challenge for the Americans.

Notably, less developed democracies tend to be less scrupulous, in today's developing world as in the nineteenth-century West. As this book was going to press, the Sri Lankan armed forces brutally demonstrated how effective counterinsurgency becomes when given a free hand. Their final campaign that crushed the Tamil insurgents started in January 2009 and employed massive, indiscriminate artillery fire. The local and international media was kept out of the combat zone, but it is assessed that over 100,000 civilians were displaced and 4,500-7,000 civilians were killed. Western powers half-heartedly criticized the Sri Lanka government, whereas Russia and China expressed support for what they proclaimed an internal affair. Massive displacement of civilian population is also taking place in the much more difficult theater of northwest Pakistan, as the Pakistani forces operate against the Taliban, in this case with the West's tacit endorsement.

The Authoritarian-Totalitarian Record of Success

It follows from our argument that nondemocratic powers ought to exhibit a substantially better record of success in curbing insurgency through the use of ruthless tactics from the late nineteenth century to the present. Needless to say, countless atrocities were committed in colonial settings by all imperial powers, irrespective of the regime. The Congo (Zaire), the private domain of King Leopold II of Belgium, was notorious for the cruel acts of coercion employed by the king's agents to force the natives to work for the rubber industry. The French brutally suppressed local resistance during their conquest of West Africa, while the British were almost as ruthless in "pacifying" Kenya, destroying crops and huts and capturing livestock to force the locals to surrender.[12]

And yet, even by colonial standards, Imperial Germany's conduct in Africa was exceptional. In German Southwest Africa, today's Namibia, the Herero revolt (1904) was countered by a policy and strategy of extermination. Wells were sealed off, and much of the population was driven out to the desert to die, while the rest were worked to death in labor camps. Only 15,000 of 80,000 Herero survived. In German East Africa, today's Tanzania, the Maji-Maji revolt (1905-1907) was similarly answered with extermination. A small force of 500 German troops destroyed settlements and crops so systematically that 250,000 to 300,000 natives died, mostly of starvation, more than 10 times the number of those who had risen in arms. The once-populous area became a wildlife reserve.[13] These were chilling demonstrations of the effectiveness of the old techniques of imperial suppression, which ultimately rested on the threat and practice of genocide.

The same spirit extended beyond Africa. To the bewilderment of public opinion in the democracies, Kaiser Wilhelm II, addressing the German troops departing to participate in the suppression of the Boxer Rebellion in China (1900), called upon them to be as merciless as Attila's Huns. German attitudes and practices in Western Europe itself had also become increasingly distinctive. Alarmed by French mass popular resistance in the latter part of the War of 1870-1871, the Germans reacted with great brutality (although hardly more so than that recommended by the American Civil War veteran General Philip Sheridan, who told Bismarck's entourage: "Nothing should be left to the people but eyes to weep with"). Harsh measures against civilian resistance were incorporated into German military manuals after 1871, and were given free rein in 1914 in widespread atrocities in Belgium, wherever the invading German troops met or imagined civilian resistance or sabotage. And if a harsh regime, as imposed by the Germans in occupied Belgium during World War I, was able to extract only partial cooperation from the Belgians, Nazi Germany's unbridled use of terror secured total compliance during World War II.[14]

Nazi Germany controlled the countries of occupied Europe and successfully harnessed them to its war economy.[15] The famous "resistance" was minimal, increasing somewhat only with the growing signs of German defeat. Only in Yugoslavia and some occupied parts of the Soviet Union did resistance in difficult terrain prove sustainable; yet there can be little doubt that had Germany won the war and been able to deploy more forces to these troublesome spots, its genocidal methods would have prevailed there, too. Imperial Japan was similarly able to subdue Taiwan (occupied in 1895), Korea (1905), and Manchuria (1931), as it very likely would have been able to accomplish throughout its "East Asian Co-prosperity Sphere," including China, had the Japanese empire survived World War II. German and Japanese imperialism was broken in the two World Wars by defeat at the hands of other great powers, rather than being dismantled under pressure from indigenous resistance in their colonies. There are no indications that resistance would have stood a chance of succeeding in their cases.

Whereas the German and Japanese imperial experiences may be regarded as too brief for the purpose of comparison, Soviet imperialism was much longer in duration. For nearly a century, the Soviet Union suppressed the peoples of the old Russian Empire—Russians and non-Russians alike—with far greater brutality than the tsars had ever employed. It did the same in the countries it had occupied in Eastern Europe during World War II, until the disintegration of the

Soviet totalitarian system for reasons other than indigenous resistance or unrest. Only in desolate Afghanistan did the invading Soviet forces fail to curb local guerilla resistance during the empire's wane, under circumstances I shall shortly discuss. Much the same applies to China, whose suppression of Tibetan and Muslim nationalism is likely to persist so long as China retains its nondemocratic regime. Thus occupied countries, including industrially developed ones permeated with a strong sense of nationalism, were controlled by and incorporated into totalitarian empires with relative ease. They were highly susceptible to ruthless pressure, to the extent that occasional demonstration rather than the actual application of such pressure was usually sufficient to keep them under the yoke.

Nonliberal powers, in other words, were less often involved in imperial wars of suppression precisely because they were so effective at suppression. Resistance was unable to grow into insurgency because it was deterred before it flared up. Because modern nondemocratic empires were held firmly under control until they were either crushed in great-power wars (as with Germany and Japan) or dismantled peacefully when the totalitarian system disintegrated (as with the Soviet Union), the sample of insurgencies is strongly biased, as it overwhelmingly comprises struggles against liberal democratic powers. The vast majority of anti-colonial insurgencies took place against liberal democratic empires—but, as Sherlock Holmes noted, it is "the dog that didn't bark" under the totalitarian iron hand that is the most conspicuous. In studies of states' war proneness, it is often forgotten that the nondemocratic imperial peace rested on successful suppression and terror. As already noted in chapter 5, the liberal democracies' greater involvement in "extra-systemic," mainly colonial, wars must be viewed in this light.

In fact, given liberal attitudes, not only "Mao's way"—violent insurgency—but also "Gandhi's way"—mass civil disobedience and demonstrations—was ultimately sufficient to force liberal powers out.

Gandhi saw very clearly that Hitlerism was supremely violent and murderous, and that it possessed none of the scruples that inhibited liberal countries. Yet he still advocated nonviolence as a method against it. He advised the Jews to opt for mass disobedience against Nazi genocidal persecution, and later offered the same advice to the occupied nations of Europe, calling on Britain to embrace civil defiance against a German invasion, in preference over armed resistance.[16] This fatuous proposal for the application of his approach only highlights the actual, unique historical and geopolitical limits within which it was able to work, and succeed—that is, when directed against liberal democratic powers.

Skeptics might question the efficacy of authoritarian-totalitarian regimes in suppressing and crushing insurgencies. The Soviet Union, did, after all, fail to subdue Afghanistan (1979-88), despite the brutal tactics that caused an estimated one million civilian dead and millions of wounded and refugees. Yet ruthlessness has always been a necessary but not sufficient condition for effective suppression. Historically, defeating irregular warfare waged by a backward and fanatical rival in a vast, desolate, and sparsely populated country, has always been a difficult undertaking. All pre-modern empires struggled with this problem. It was largely in this context that the Soviet Union failed to win the war in Afghanistan, just as the British had failed to do in the nineteenth century, while easily controlling India. The insurgents' ability to take refuge across the border in neighboring Pakistan significantly contributed to the Soviet failure, as it presently complicates matters for the Americans. Yet this failure also signaled deep problems developing within the Soviet system that would shortly lead to its collapse, including a certain loss of nerve in employing the Stalinist-type brutality that was essential for the survival of such a regime. Under Stalin, the Soviet Union evinced no scruples in resorting to the classical technique for eradicating popular resistance, deporting whole populations (including the Chechens) *en masse* from their homelands. Popular resistance in the Ukraine and the Baltic countries prior to and following World War II was similarly crushed by the harshest of measures, occasionally escalating into a strategy of extermination. Afghanistan was the exception—or "outlier"—in the Soviet imperial system. It is no coincidence that the secession of the former Soviet republics, as well as the insurgency in Chechnya, took place only after the breakdown of the Soviet system. Furthermore, whereas the liberalizing Russia of the 1990s was forced to give in to the Chechen insurgents, the Russia that has been turning in a more authoritarian direction has proved tenacious in curbing this resistance by ruthless means. The order on the scale is unmistakable: Soviet methods under Stalin were the most brutal and most effective in curbing resistance, while Putin's Russia constitutes an intermediate case, with a liberalizing Russia of the 1990s proving the least brutal and least effective. One reason for Russia's backtracking from liberalism was a growing sense in the country that the application of liberal norms would result not merely in the dissolution of the Soviet bloc and the Soviet Union but would also threaten the territorial integrity of the Russian Federation itself.

Like Nazi Germany (especially after the outbreak of World War II), wartime Imperial Japan, and Mao's China, Stalin's Soviet Union cared very little about opinion in the liberal West. In other times and cases, however, the power and wealth of the liberal sphere has exerted at least some measure of constraint on those less brutal and less inward-looking nonliberal regimes that felt sufficiently dependent on cooperation with the liberal countries to pay some heed to their sensibilities. Since the beginning of the nineteenth century, even nonliberal countries have been working in the context of an international system in which liberal countries and liberal public opinion carry weight and must be taken into account. Napoleonic France is an interesting early example, for it already operated within the constraints and norms of an enlightened Europe to which France had contributed so significantly and which the Empire proudly claimed to represent. Even that rare case of judicial killing under the First Consul, the abduction and execution of the Duke d'Enghien (1804)—which is trifling by the standards of twentieth-century totalitarianism—was greeted with an outcry and condemnation both at home and abroad. Thus, despite the widespread atrocities committed by both sides during the savage war in the Iberian Peninsula (those by the French were graphically depicted by Goya), Napoleon did not resort to the semi-genocidal methods that had been used by the Romans in their long struggle to "pacify" that same difficult arena, though the Spanish ulcer was causing his empire to hemorrhage. Like the various circles of hell, there are degrees of brutality, and there is a hell of a difference between them. Though Soviet methods in Afghanistan and Russian methods in Chechnya were brutal by Western liberal standards, they still fall far short of the genocidal methods used by a Hitler or a Stalin to curb resistance and crush insurgency.

Finally, skeptics might argue that while the Americans encountered all the familiar problems in their counterinsurgency war in Iraq (where everybody had been kept ruthlessly in check by Saddam Hussein), they have been relatively more successful in Afghanistan than the Soviets had. Indeed, these American experiences highlight some preconditions for the success of liberal democracies in irregular wars. These include (a) the ability to apply their massive superiority in high-tech warfare, which is far more attuned to targeting hardware than people, but which was more freely employed in the Afghan deserts than in Iraq's urban spaces; and (b) the availability of a strong enough indigenous allied force on the ground to be able to establish authority and shoulder the dirty work of land warfare and occupation. Such a force existed in Afghanistan initially but was missing at the beginning in Iraq, though the situation may be reversing itself in these countries—with predictable results.

Conclusion

Counterinsurgency warfare's record of failure turns out to be mainly the lot of modern liberal democracies—arising, in fact, from their noblest of traits. This is generally obscured by the West's self-criticism and the rhetoric of decolonization. For all of liberal colonialism's abuses and brutality (as well as its often-forgotten blessings), resistance to colonialism succeeded overwhelmingly against liberal democratic powers. Ultimately, such powers found enforced rule over others to be too starkly at variance with their most fundamental values of freedom, equality, and self-government; the traditional atrocious means against civilians of effective counterinsurgency were unacceptable; and the majority of the territories in question were expendable or susceptible to successful incorporation into the liberal economic sphere, even with an end to direct rule. None of these considerations affected the authoritarian and totalitarian powers that crushed resistance with an iron fist, as they continue to do.[17]

This is not to say that the democracies always lose counterinsurgency wars, while nondemocracies always win. Democracies can succeed when they are able to isolate the insurgents from the civilian population and when pressed to the wall. But overall they find dealing with counterinsurgency highly problematic. Weak authoritarian regimes have sometimes failed in counterinsurgency conflicts because of their weakness, but strong authoritarian regimes, and especially totalitarian ones, rarely fail. Other factors are surely involved in each particular case, but the record is heavily tilted against democracies in such struggles.

Needless to say, the constraints on the use of ruthless means against civilians remain in force in liberal democratic powers, and only fringe groups within them suggest that they should be eliminated. The other reasons for the liberal democracies' poor record in fighting irregulars also retain most of their validity. This suggests that the democracies' performance in such struggles is unlikely to improve dramatically, with all the resulting implications. Even when the moral case is viewed as imperative in liberal eyes, as in humanitarian interventions and peace-keeping missions aimed at stopping mass killings, action is likely to fail, or simply be deterred, when at least one of the local sides opposes it and adopts persistent irregular warfare. After the fiascos of international intervention in Lebanon (1982-1983) and Somalia (1992-1994), nobody was willing to act in the cases of Rwanda and Darfur. The international force dispatched to southern Lebanon in the wake of the 2006 war is likely to remain in place and prove partly effective in preventing a full-scale Hezbullah return only so long as Hezbullah chooses not to challenge it, for reasons having to do with domestic Lebanese politics, the balance of terror vis-à-vis Israel, and regional considerations concerning Iran and Syria.

But this is not all. The hallmark of the New World Disorder is the emergence of new vital security concerns, largely emanating from previously ignorable colonial and post-colonial societies. With nuclear proliferation and the biotechnological revolution, the trickling down of weapons of mass destruction to below the state level has become a real and terrifying prospect, involving non-state actors against whom deterrence is ineffective (see chapter 9), and who are often nestled within broadly sympathetic civilian populations. Thus the problem of fighting irregulars successfully has returned with a vengeance, and it remains as intractable as before.

In all likelihood, if a nuclear device were ever set off in a major Western city, or a "super-bug" developed in a clandestine laboratory were released to cause mass death, democracies would react with far fewer constraints than they have in the past—adopting means far in excess of even the controversial post-9/11 measures. Short of this doomsday scenario, more emphasis should be put on the above-mentioned factors for success.

In the first place, there is still an unfulfilled potential in the adaptation of high-tech warfare to the task of fighting irregulars. Israel (whose rivals are more geographically identifiable) and the United States have increasingly invested in surveillance, tracking, and robotic systems designed to detect and dig out low-signature irregulars operating in a dense civilian environment. To be sure, though, the limitations of too-clinical high-tech measures were demonstrated by Israel's less than successful 2006 encounter with Hezbullah.*

Second, as far as possible, democracies should cultivate indigenous allies who enjoy greater local legitimacy than does a foreign power, are more familiar with the local populations, and are also less constrained in their conduct. The Sunni tribal leaders whose cooperation is the main reason for the weakening of al-Qaeda in Iraq, and the moderate, pro-Western, semi-autocratic state leaderships in the Arab world are obvious examples. The removal of President Pervez Musharraf of Pakistan in 2008 by the new democratic government that appears to be less collaborative—and successful—in suppressing militant Islamists demonstrates the pros and cons of such a policy, which must be decided on a case by case basis. Its limited effectiveness in some circumstances, as well as the moral dilemmas involved, are part of the deal. But as long as it can be made to work, war-by-proxy is far more effective than foreign intervention.

Even unfriendly state regimes usually constitute a better option than no regime at all or a wholesale foreign intervention. Because when all other means fail, military coercion against states, with their vulnerable infrastructures, tends to be far more effective than counterinsurgency. NATO's aerial action against Serbia in the 1999 Kosovo war and the U.S. blockade of, and aerial operations against, Iraq before the 2003 invasion were tailored to avoid the kinds of mil-

---

* After writing this, I was interested to read in Bob Woodward's book, *The War Within: A Secret White House History, 2006-2008* (2008), that more than the rise in troops' number, it was the collaboration of the Sunni tribal leaders and, most intriguingly, secret new developments in American intelligence and striking technologies against terrorists—"as secretive as the Manhattan project"—that accounted for the steep decline in terrorist activity in Iraq.

itary involvement at which liberal democracies are weakest. These measures, too, such as blockade and the targeting of vital and capital-intensive infrastructure, hurt the civilian population, sometimes hard, and have been criticized in liberal democracies on moral and legal grounds. Yet when adequate precautions are taken, the killing of and hardships placed on civilians can be significantly reduced.

Of course, when vital interests are involved and indigenous state authorities either do not exist or are unable to enforce their authority, counterinsurgency tactics on the ground may still prove necessary, revealing the liberal democracies at both their best and weakest.

8
Did Democracies Exterminate the Natives of North America and Australia?

The liberal democracies' colonial record includes a particularly problematic element: the charge that in both the United States and Australia, democracies exterminated the native populations. This is the source of a profound sense of guilt in the two countries, reinforcing pervasive doubts about whether liberal democratic societies really behave better than others. Leading historical sociologist Michael Mann develops the charge of genocide in his book *The Dark Side of Democracy: Explaining Ethnic Cleansing* (2004). Mann regards it as a major flaw in the democratic peace proposition. But this charge is fundamentally invalid, as are the conclusions derived from it.

Mann's main thesis is that murderous ethnic cleansing, which in extreme forms can become genocidal, is predominantly a modern phenomenon. It is the "dark side of democracy," when the rule of the people and the ethnicity of the people are "confused," In premodern times, class prevailed over ethnicity in the eyes of conquerors and social elites, who sought to subjugate and exploit people irrespective of their ethnic identity, rather than get rid of them. However, the advent of modernity, popular sovereignty, and universal citizenship occasionally spurred violence between rival ethnic groups that claimed the same territory. In extreme cases, their struggles escalated into murderous ethnic cleansing and even genocide.

We begin our scrutiny of this thesis with the premodern world. Was murderous ethnic cleansing rare then? As revealed by recent scholarship, prehistoric conflict between small human groups often resulted in massacre and even extermination. A singular example is the spread of our species, *homo sapiens*, out of Africa an estimated 70,000 years ago. In that process, all the archaic humans who inhabited the Old World were gradually extinguished, everywhere displaced and replaced, victims of what was probably our species' superior skills in subsisting, reproducing, and fighting. Incidentally, there is no need to shift the blame for murderous mass killing from our civilization to our species, a popular holdover from the 1960s. As viewers of television nature documentaries witness, high rates of intra-killing within animal species are the norm in nature.

Another example may be the displacement and replacement of the earliest inhabitants of what is present-day Japan by the population now known as Japanese. The Japanese apparently arrived from Korea in around 300 BC, bringing wet rice agriculture with them. They gradually pushed the earlier, Jamon, inhabitants up the archipelago through a combination of numbers, dense agricultural settlement, and warfare. Today only about 150,000 of the remnant of the Jamon, the Ainu, live in Hokkaido and other northern islands. And this is merely one example of many from the shadowy light of prehistory.

We now move from prehistory to history, when states, stratified societies, and elite rule dominated. This is an era that is far more central to Mann's argument. He notes the massive killing, massacre, razing of cities, and mass uprooting of populations that were very much the stuff of history. He mentions some well-known examples from the wars of Assyria, Greece, Rome, Carthage, the Anglo-Saxon invasion of Britain, and the exploits of nomadic hordes such as the Mongols. As he correctly states, "Warfare occasionally strayed into ethnocide." All the same, Mann insists that since economic exploitation by a ruling and often ethnically foreign elite was the rationale of premodern society, such brutality should be regarded as marginal. According to this logic, the conquering and ruling elites resorted to vicious means to suppress and/or set an example for others as quickly and efficiently as possible, with the aim of resuming exploitation with the least possible disturbance.

But this attractive model is misleading. For one thing, enslavement was always one of the main options of exploitation, and not only in the figurative sense of subjugating people in and on their land, but also in the ordinary sense (which Mann barely mentions) of taking them as captives and selling them far away from home. This was standard practice in military operations, often constituting the main booty. Occasionally, conquering armies emptied cities and bled white provinces. Indeed, we sometimes hear of the price of slaves falling in the markets on account of the massive supply. Africa, of course, furnishes an especially gruesome example: tens of millions of people were carried north through the Sahara and out of East Africa by Arab and Muslim slave traders well before Europeans began the trade from West Africa. Both Arabs and Europeans collaborated with native polities that provided the slaves through raids and wars against their neighbors. Thus ethnic cleansing was economically motivated well before modernity.

Furthermore, the model that Mann seems to have in mind is that of imperial wars. However, routine warlike activity in history was much more mundane, taking place between neighboring small-scale polities and driven by a variety of motives that most often included capturing border land. While the victors grabbed and settled on the land, the indigenous population typically fled rather than waiting to be looted, enslaved, driven away, or killed. In most cases, such small polities did not have the capability to rule over one another, and on the rare occasions that one of them succeeded in conquering a long-time neighbor and rival, it more characteristically razed it to the ground. If "macro-ethnic cleansing" was rare in premodern times, it is because macro-ethnicities and macro-states themselves were rarer; murderous "micro-ethnic cleansing" took place all the time.

So ethnic cleansing, involving widespread massacres, mass destruction of settlements, mass enslavement, and masses of refugees driven out by war, were commonplace in premodern times—probably more so than in modern times. All the same, Mann may still have a point in claiming that modern ethnic cleansing is somehow different, possessing a special quality that distinguishes it from earlier examples. As he sees it, democracy is the new development that begot ethnic cleansing. His point would carry some validity, but for the strange meanings he attaches to the concept of democracy.

It is true that spreading notions of popular sovereignty and equal universal citizenship made the peaceful existence of ethnically foreign people within a state more problematic, and prompted deep tensions and violence. The growth of popular sovereignty, the institutionalization of universal citizenship, the creation of mass society, and deepening popular mobilization are sometimes reasonably labeled democratization. Some scholars of nationalism point out their connection to the rise of nationalism, although many consider it anathema. There was no confusion here between the political and ethnic meanings of the concept of the people, as Mann would have it, criticizing President Wilson, for example, for committing such a category mistake; rather, as people's involvement in the public sphere increased, they exhibited a strong preference for political self-identification and self-determination in concert with their ethnic kin. That preference has profoundly and often violently affected both domestic and international politics during the past two centuries. In this sense, then, democratization and nationalism have gone hand in hand. However, whereas popular sovereignty, universal citizenship, mass society, and popular mobilization can be labeled democratization, they cannot be equated with democracy, a far more restricted phenomenon, without stretching the latter term to the breaking point. The great majority of state societies that underwent these processes did not become democratic, unless the term is indiscriminately applied to a whole range of repressive and often atrocious authoritarian and totalitarian regimes.

Mann examines a series of ethnic cleansing and genocide cases during the nineteenth and twentieth centuries that he surprisingly attributes to democracy: ethnic expulsions and massacres in the nondemocratic Balkans before and after the First World War; Czarist Russia's treatment of Muslims in the conquered Caucasus; the genocide of the Armenians in the Ottoman Empire under the authoritarian-nationalist Young Turks; the deportation of Germans from post-World War II Eastern Europe; and the events in the democratizing former Yugoslavia and Rwanda during the 1990s. Even more surprisingly, he also includes in the list of democratic ethnic cleansing the Nazi genocide of the Jews and their actual and planned treatment of the Slavs, as well as communist cleansings, mass killings, and genocides under Stalin in the Soviet Union, Mao in China, and Pol Pot in Cambodia. In Mann's terminology there are "liberal democracies" and "ethnic democracies," with Nazi Germany belonging to the latter type. The accepted distinction is actually between liberal or civic nationalism and ethnic nationalism. Although this distinction has its problems, it is less confusing and it more clearly indicates the real culprit: militant nationalism.

Of course, the totalitarian socialist countries such as Russia, China, and Cambodia can hardly be classified as ethnic democracies, so Mann further overstretches his thesis by claiming that Stalin, Mao, and Pol Pot in fact carried out their class persecution and elimination in the name of a class identified as "The People," and thus fall under the category of democratic (and ethnic?) cleansing. This explanation recalls the old designations of these totalitarian socialist regimes as "people's republics" and "democratic republics."

Why would an able sociologist like Mann tie himself in such strange knots? It is because he believes that not only "ethnic democracies" but also liberal democracies strayed into ethnic cleansing in colonial-frontier settings. He alleges that genocidal democracies were responsible for "the most successful cleansing the world may have ever seen": the United States targeted the Native Americans and Australia the Aboriginals. Both indigenous groups were displaced from their lands and experienced, respectively, an estimated 90 percent and 80 percent drop in numbers during the nineteenth and early twentieth centuries. Mann concedes that well-established democracies do not carry out murderous ethnic cleansing, but claims that in earlier, more formative stages of their development they did.

To be sure, both Native Americans and Aboriginal Australians were victims of massive expropriation and their violent resistance was suppressed by the more effective violence of governments and local white settlers. The land on which the natives lived was progressively taken from them, devastating their livelihood and way of life. The United States carried out some large-scale and deadly deportations, such as that of the Cherokees, and local militias, most notably in California, engaged in indiscriminate killings. Small-scale violence and killings were pervasive. Native women were occasionally taken away and raped by white men. The natives' lives, well-being, and culture were horribly damaged. Most of the white population saw the natives as a menace to be defeated, as did the authorities, more so in the independent republic of the United States than in colonial Australia. The greatest presidents of democratic America—George Washington, Thomas Jefferson, Andrew Jackson, Abraham Lincoln, Theodore Roosevelt—prophesized the natives' ultimate doom, which they believed to be much-deserved in light of natives' acts of savage violence. All this is undeniably true. Hence people tend to assume the worst. Nonetheless, the demographic ca-

tastrophe that befell the Native Americans and Aboriginal Australians was not caused by such means. The culprit was very different, and it struck indiscriminate of intent and regime type.

The source of the natives' demographic calamity in both the
Americas and Australia was their lack of immunity to Old World diseases, including smallpox, measles, influenza, typhus, and tuberculo-
sis. Most of these diseases had passed from domesticated livestock to
humans during the Neolithic agricultural revolution and spread
through the population of the Old World, which in time had developed resistance to them. The sudden joining of the Old and New
Worlds spelled disaster for the natives of the latter, as the diseases
migrated across the oceans with the European newcomers. Mann
clearly presents the consequences of the ensuing biological holocaust,
affirming the now prevailing view that it caused the death of some
90 percent of the pre-contact native population throughout the
Americas. He well recognizes that this horrific death toll was unin-
tentional, rightly regarding the well-known sporadic cases in which
contaminated blankets and cloths were deliberately given to the natives to precipitate their demise as inconsequential to the general,
practically unstoppable, trend. All the same, while writing at great
length about everything else, he devotes only a couple of pages to
this factor, practically ignoring the implications of that devastating
development for his argument.

But how can we determine precisely what part of the demise of
these native populations was due to epidemic diseases and what part
to human brutality? In history and the social sciences, where events
cannot be replayed, the only means of answering such questions is
through controlled comparisons. Mann argues correctly that in both
the United States and Australia, where farmer settlement was the
norm, the farmers had little use for the natives and were particularly
interested in seeing them gone. For this reason, he believes, the frontier democracy practiced by settlers was the most atrocious toward

the natives. But what, then, can we learn from other places, where the relevant circumstances were different?

Let us begin with colonial Spanish America, which was not democratic, of course. Furthermore, the Spanish conquistadores in the early sixteenth century were quintessentially premodern in Mann's sense: they exhibited great ruthlessness during their conquests and suppressed and abused the natives, but they wanted them to live so that they could be exploited. They needed the natives to work for them in mines and on landed estates or plantations—the common agricultural possession in Spanish America. However, the natives of the Caribbean, where the Spanish first landed and established their rule, died of European diseases at such a fast rate that they were wiped out altogether. The Spaniards saw no alternative but to import African slaves, who despite great mortality rates during ocean crossings and horrible abuse over centuries thereafter, survived in great numbers in the Americas because of their natural resistance to Old World epidemic diseases.

Much the same applies to the rest of Spanish America, where European diseases were a major factor in the destruction of the Aztec and Inca empires, killing an estimated half of each population, including the emperors at the time of conquest. The common estimate now is that within a century after the conquest, the native population fell by about 90 percent and then slowly recovered in the following centuries, after the people gradually developed resistance to the new diseases. The natives of Amazonia, isolated until recently, have been much abused over the past generation by entrepreneurs and their workforces penetrating the rain forests to carry out large-scale projects of economic development. Above all, however, their lives are threatened by contact with European diseases, whose deadly effects are today preventable by large-scale immunization.

We now turn to North America. A dense agricultural-urban civilization existed in the Mississippi River Valley, but a Spanish probing expedition led by Hernando De Soto observed in 1540 that its towns were deserted. This native civilization is believed to have succumbed to European diseases that spread from Mexico even before its contact with the Europeans, let alone with white settlers. When the English and French arrived at the same area in the following centuries, this civilization was already long gone. The same terrible process took place throughout North America, as contact and disease gradually spread across the continent. Sparse native populations, rather than falling victim to genocide, were afflicted each in turn by disease brought in by the settlers. Most native populations reached their lowest point some 100 years after contact. The natives of California suffered a disastrous decline, to an estimated half of their pre-contact population, under Spanish and Mexican rule and the mission and estate system. Their numbers continued to fall with the advent of American rule—again only minimally due to direct killings, cruel and indiscriminate as they were. The natives of Pennsylvania and New Jersey were sheltered from harassment by the Quaker communities alongside which they lived; this did not, however, prevent their virtual elimination by disease.

One last control case is that of French Algeria. The atrocious treatment of black Africans in America did not cause blacks to decline demographically—quite the opposite; nor did colonial abuse in black Africa itself in the nineteenth and twentieth centuries have that effect, except for a few cases of direct genocide, such as those perpetrated by imperial Germany (discussed in the previous chapter). In North Africa, too, French occupation and settlement of Algeria after 1830 involved ferocious "pacification" of native resistance. Nevertheless, during the very same period in which the native North American population was plummeting, Algeria's population actually surged, from some 2.5 million in 1800 to about 6 million in 1920.

Thus an examination of Mann's independent variables—democracy and the "frontier democracy" of farmer settlers—in diverse cases across historical experience belies his contention about democracies' track record. This is not to say that the natives of America and Australia were not treated harshly and often atrociously. The advance of dense agricultural settlement forced them from their land and disrupted their livelihoods, their way of life, and their culture. They experienced blatant discrimination and were subject to deadly deportations and killings. These purposeful acts contributed to their disasters, but did not—could not—cause them. More generally, it is true that popular sovereignty, universal citizenship, mass popular mobilization, and mass society—which can be labeled democratization—made nationalism more manifest and, consequently, added a new dimension to ethnic tensions and cleansing. It is also true that liberal democracies' standards for the treatment of ethnic minorities in colonial settings were very different from those they practiced at home, and were sometimes harsh. Liberal democratic standards rose dramatically during the nineteenth and twentieth centuries. Still, it takes ideological zealotry, which leads to fundamental errors in argument and method, to label ethnic cleansing as the dark side of democracy.

9
Unconventional Terror and the New World Disorder

The September 11, 2001, mega-terror attacks in New York City and Washington D.C. were a historical landmark not only because of their direct and indirect consequences but also because they demonstrated an ominous potential that had been building for some time and has yet to be fully realized. The attacks came as a surprise, and far-reaching precautions were adopted only in their wake. But experts and governmental authorities had recognized this potential from the late 1980s. It was the subject of Congressional investigations and legislation, and was highlighted by President Clinton and his Defense Secretary William Cohen. Yet it continues to be denied and misunderstood by many. This is the threat of unconventional terror that employs so-called weapons of mass destruction (WMD)—nuclear, biological, and chemical.

The Threat

Neither terror nor weapons of mass destruction is entirely new. Terror—the targeting of civilians for political purposes by small, non-state groups—is widely claimed to have existed throughout history.[1] More accurately, however, while the assassination of leaders is as old as humanity, terror only emerged in the late nineteenth century on the heels of modern technological and social developments: high explosives and, later, automatic weapons gave individuals and small groups the unprecedented ability to cause damage disproportionate to their number; trains and then cars gave them mobility across countries; telegraph communication and popular newspapers gave their operations national publicity and resonance that vastly magnified the public terror effect of what in fact were very limited actions. This was the material underpinning of the emergence of anarchist terrorism in Russia and the rest of Europe in the late nineteenth century, and anti-colonial terror in the twentieth.

Again, it was mainly liberal and old-style authoritarian countries that proved the most susceptible to terror. Totalitarian countries not only policed far more effectively but also denied terror the publicity essential for its success. Beginning in the 1960s, terror experienced a surge, as passenger jets offered both greater global mobility and vulnerable targets, and as television further enhanced the terrorists' public exposure. Yet it is only the prospect of terrorists acquiring and using weapons of mass destruction that has turned terrorism from an irritant and a media-political tool into a serious destructive threat, thereby producing the alarming twist of the new era.

The so-called weapons of mass destruction are an assortment of technologies with widely diverging potency. The potential use of chemical weapons by terrorists is predicated on the element of surprise, catching masses of people unprotected and therefore highly vulnerable in an open urban space. However, chemical weapons pose the least serious threat of the WMDs because of the high volume of chemical agents needed and the problem of spreading them effectively and undetected with the means terrorists might possess. A highly successful chemical terror attack is estimated to have a casualty rate in the thousands.

Biological weapons pose a threat of a much greater magnitude. Strains of bacteria and viruses currently regarded as particularly potent in terms of lethality, resistance to medication, and persistence in the environment include anthrax, plague, tularemia, typhoid fever, cholera, typhus, Q fever, smallpox, and Ebola. Toxins such as botulinum and ricin also carry the potential for mass killing. Throughout history, big epidemics were much greater killers than wars, with a virulent strain of influenza killing an estimated 20 million to 40 million people worldwide in 1918-1919—more than died during all of World War I. Since then, medicine has conquered infectious diseases. However, the revolutionary breakthroughs during recent decades in decoding the genome, in biotechnology, and in genetic engineering have made biological weapons much more lethal and accessible. A virulent laboratory-cultivated strain of bacteria or virus, let alone a specially-engineered "superbug" with no immunological or medical antidote,[2] could make biological weapons as lethal as nuclear attacks, and result in anywhere from thousands to many millions of fatalities. At the same time, they are far more easily available to terrorists than nuclear weapons.

Still, nuclear weapons are in a category all their own. Not only is their destructive power so great that a large enough nuclear stockpile could destroy any rival; there is also no effective defense against them even remotely commensurate with their destructiveness. In the absence of effective defense again nuclear weapons, mutual deterrence became the dominant strategic rationale, and has prevented a nuclear war—and perhaps any war between nuclear states—since 1945. Herein lies the bewildering danger of the new unconventional terror: deterrence is infinitely less effective against terrorist groups than it is against states. Not only are such groups more likely to consist of extremist zealots willing to sacrifice their own lives and even positively desiring a general apocalypse; they are also too elusive to offer a clear enough target for retaliation, on which the whole concept of deterrence is based.

The root of the problem lies in the way the technologies and materials of WMD are trickling down below the state level. Chemical, biological, and nuclear facilities for both civilian and military use have vastly proliferated worldwide over the past decades. The relatively simple technological infrastructure needed for the manufacture of chemical weapons is now available in some 100 countries,[3] and is also within reach of non-state groups. The biotechnology sector in particular has been at the forefront of revolutionary developments in science and products for the consumer market. By the late 1990s, there were already an estimated 1,300 biotechnology companies in the United States and 580 in Europe.[4] One estimate suggests there are some 20,000 labs in the world, where, within the next decade, a single person will be able to synthesize any existing virus. In the same labs, five people with $2 million will be able to create an enhanced pathogen—a virus that could infect and kill people who have been immunized with conventional vaccines. With $5 million, the same five people could build a lab from scratch, using equipment purchased online.[5] In the U.S. alone, the number of scientists authorized to work with biological agents has risen sharply, to 15,000, creating huge challenges for government monitors.[6] As markets and communications rapidly globalize, it has become far easier to acquire the materials, equipment, and know-how required for WMD, while it has become far more difficult to detect and block such acquisitions. The necessary equipment and materials often have dual uses, and can be purchased for ostensibly benign civilian purposes. Finally, the disintegration of the Soviet Union left in the debris of its advanced military infrastructure, spread throughout its various former republics, an array of unemployed scientists, production facilities, unaccounted-for and poorly-guarded materials that can be made into weapons, and, most worrying, the weapons themselves. For these reasons, terrorists' ability to buy, steal, or manufacture WMD has increased dramatically.

To be sure, the practical difficulties facing terrorist groups that wish to follow the unconventional path are still considerable. In

1990-1995, the Aum Shinrikyo cult in Japan was the first non-state group to build production facilities for biological and chemical weapons. The group was immensely wealthy and included trained scientists and hundreds of engineers. It purchased the necessary machines and materials worldwide, many of them on the open market. It produced and used botulinum toxin and anthrax, but when results proved unsatisfactory, probably due to low quality material, it concentrated on nerve gases, particularly sarin. The cult struggled with acute safety problems in the production process because of the high toxicity and corrosiveness of the biological and chemical agents. Nonetheless, it went on with production and carried out roughly 10 biological and 10 chemical attacks. The largest of them was a sarin attack in the Tokyo subway in 1995. Although thousands of people required medical treatment, only 12 died. The low fatality rate was due mainly to the low quality of the sarin and the primitive mechanism for its dissemination (plastic bags pierced by umbrellas). All the same, when the police closed in on the cult and its facilities, it was working on manufacturing more effective spraying mechanisms and 70 tons of sarin, while also building a large biological laboratory.[7]

Similarly, the long-unresolved anthrax attack in the United States in the wake of September 11, now attributed to a scientist in the U.S. biological warfare laboratory who committed suicide in July 2008, involved anthrax delivered in envelopes sent through the U.S. postal service. The attack killed five people and created panic, contaminated entire buildings, and shut down facilities. While the scientist, Bruce Ivins, seems to have been mentally disturbed and his motives remain unclear, he probably did not want to cause mass death. However, aerosolized anthrax that is sprayed effectively can cause a disaster of an entirely different order of magnitude. According to a Congressional assessment made as early as 1993, a light plane flying over Washington, D.C., and spraying 100 kilograms of anthrax could kill three million people. Thus, despite major difficulties and limited successes, the first sarin and anthrax terror attacks represent only the tip of the iceberg of the potential threat posed by chemical and biological terrorism, especially as the biotechnology revolution is only beginning to unfold.

In contrast, terrorists have not yet used nuclear weapons, and they cannot produce fissile material, at least for the foreseeable future. All the same, terrorists can use stolen or purchased radioactive materials to create a radioactive bomb. Though it would not compare with a nuclear weapon in destructiveness, such a "dirty bomb" could contaminate entire city blocks with radioactivity that is exceedingly difficult to remove. Moreover, several tests carried out by scientists for American authorities found that a nuclear bomb can be built from parts available on the open market, with fissile material that is bought or stolen. Nuclear weapons themselves might be stolen or bought on the black market, and not even very expensively. Abdul Qadeer Khan, the Pakistani nuclear scientist who headed his country's program to manufacture an atomic bomb, sold the nuclear secrets to perhaps a dozen countries—from Southeast Asia to the Middle East, including North Korea, Iran, and Libya—reportedly for as little as millions or tens of millions of dollars. The price of a bomb itself—purchased, for example, in the republics of the former Soviet Union, possibly with the help of organized crime—might be just as low.

As Rolf Mowatt-Larssen, the U.S. Energy Department's director of intelligence, told the Washington Post's David Ignatius, al-Qaeda was seeking to acquire weapons of mass destruction for nearly a decade before September 11. Osama bin Laden offered $1.5 million to buy uranium for a nuclear device. In August 2001, just before the attack on the U.S., bin Laden and his deputy, Ayman al-Zawahiri, met with Pakistani scientists to discuss how al-Qaeda could build such a device. Al-Qaeda also had an aggressive anthrax program that was discovered in December 2001, after the organization was driven from Afghanistan. In 2003, Saudi operatives of al-Qaeda tried to buy three Russian nuclear bombs. Around the same time, Zawahiri decided to cancel a cyanide attack in the New York subway system, telling the plotters to stand down because "we have something better in mind." After 2004, al-Qaeda's WMD trail went cold.[8] Even more than with Aum Shinrikyo, the price of al-Qaeda's successful terror attack on 9/11 may have been to nip its far more dangerous plans in the bud. It seems clear that the loss of the Afghani safe haven was a serious blow to al-Qaeda's WMD program, though, of course, the price of success is that we shall probably never know for certain. The failure of al-Qaeda to initiate further terrorist acts on U.S. soil after 9/11 (pointed out by those who believe that the danger has been exaggerated) is largely attributable to the loss of that safe haven. As with other effective countermeasures, the problem of the "dog that didn't bark" re-surfaces and should not become a cause for complacency.

For much of history, non-state players such as tribal and armed gang leaders challenged states successfully. With modernity, states' dominance increased as they increasingly controlled the heavy infrastructure underlying power. Although states still dominate, despite encroachments from various directions, the encapsulation of destructive power in WMD, particularly nuclear and biological, recreates a situation in which a player no longer has to be big in order to deliver a devastating punch. World-threatening individuals and organizations, previously the preserve of James Bond-style fiction, have suddenly become real.

Some have argued in the wake of September 11 that it is wrong to define terror as the enemy, because terror is only a tactic, whereas the enemy is militant Islam. True, radical Islam stands behind most terrorist attacks in today's world, and dealing with it is an intricate and complex problem. Yet, although this new challenge is labeled as fascist, the Arab and Muslim societies from which it arises are generally poor and stagnant. They represent no alternative model for the future and pose no military threat to the developed liberal democratic world, as did the fascist great powers, which were among the world's strongest and most advanced societies, or as the new capitalist nondemocratic giants may. Only the potential use of WMD makes the threat of militant Islam significant. Furthermore, even if the problem of militant Islam were overcome, other causes and "super-empowered angry men" (as New York Times columnist Thomas Friedman has called them) would always be present and, in contrast to the past, could now assert themselves with horrific consequences. The Aum Shinrikyo cult, anthrax scientist Bruce Ivins, and the perpetrators of the massive conventional bombings in Oklahoma City (1995) and the Atlanta Olympics (1996) were not Muslim. While societies in general can become more pacific, as through the affluent liberal democratic path, there will always be individuals and small groups who will embrace massive violence for some cause. Thus unconventional terror *is* the problem.

The leveling effect of nuclear weapons has long been discussed. But it was always considered with respect to relations between states, with an otherwise weak side possessing a nuclear retaliatory capability able to deter the strong side from war. Now, however, terror groups that possess an unconventional capability may benefit from a similar equalizing effect in their relations with states, but without the constraints of mutual deterrence. To be sure, unconventional terror groups are still likely to be much weaker than states. A chemical attack that would kill thousands might be considered a trifle in comparison to the human cost of a serious interstate war or even to the numbers killed each year in road accidents. However, biological or nuclear weapons, whose killing potential is much greater, may cause a disaster on a par with the United States' most severe wars; and who now can say with any confidence that such an attack is not feasible? Indeed, because deterrence based on mutual assured destruction

(MAD) does not apply to terrorists, terrorists are *more* likely than states are to use the ultimate weapons, though the latter may possess far greater unconventional capability. In contrast to the habits of mind that dominated since the onset of the nuclear age, unconventional capability acquired by terrorists is *useable*. If only because of the technical problems involved, unconventional terror is likely to be used in relatively few cases and will undoubtedly continue to constitute only a small minority of all terrorist attacks. Yet, once the potential is available, it is difficult to see what will stop it from being realized by someone, somewhere.

Terrorist groups may work from within their target countries, smuggling in or even manufacturing unconventional weapons undetected by the authorities. The Aum Shinrikyo cult in Japan built its facilities for the manufacture of biological and chemical agents undetected in one of the world's most advanced countries. The whole phenomenon was homegrown. The perpetrators of the September 11 conventional mega-terror attacks trained in the United States and other Western countries. In separate incidences in 2003, British and French police raided residences where Islamic extremist were preparing ricin and botulinum toxins from chemical materials ordered on the open market. The notion of "a bomb in the basement," originally conceived in relation to states' undeclared development of nuclear weapons, has acquired a chilling new meaning.

The problem is even greater with respect to countries in the developing world. Not only can terrorists find a safe haven for their activities in militant or failed states; these countries are also a source for dangerous materials and weapons, because of their low security standards and high levels of corruption. Indeed, failed states may constitute as great or even greater a problem than militant ones. Although some militant regimes, most notably the Taliban, have demonstrated little concern for the massive retaliation that would follow acts of mega-terror originating from their territory, others are likely to be more susceptible to deterrence. By contrast, weak or failed states simply do not exercise effective control over their territories and cannot be effectively held accountable. In vast and largely inaccessible tracts of the globe inhabited by fragmented and unruly societies, monitoring and cracking down on the activity of terrorist groups may be harder than finding a needle in a haystack.

The Response

All these are baffling problems, which do not lend themselves to easy or clear solutions. Still, the most feasible measure against unconventional terror is a coordinated global crackdown, which includes tightened security measures, tougher controls on the materials and facilities for the production of weapons of mass destruction, and the relentless pursuit of terrorists.[9] Though haggling and conflicts of interest are sure to arise, such concerted action is not wholly utopian, for no state is immune to the threat. Nautical piracy was thus eliminated in the nineteenth century, with the British hegemon playing the major role in naval policing and in fostering cooperation. And the stakes with respect to unconventional terror are much higher. International norms and international law are likely to change in response to the new challenges, most notably, perhaps, with respect to the question of sovereignty.

The greatest obstacle to the success of a policy of global crackdown is the proliferation of WMD—above all, nuclear weapons. The 187 countries that have joined the Nuclear Non-Proliferation Treaty (NPT) have agreed not to develop nuclear weapons and have accepted an inspection regime carried out by the International Atomic Energy Agency (IAEA). As a result, the nuclear club has grown only modestly and now includes the five authorized members (the United States, Russia, China, Britain, and France), plus India, Pakistan, Israel (undeclared), and North Korea (possibly). South

Africa voluntarily disarmed itself of the nuclear capability built during its apartheid regime. Iraq and Libya gave up their programs through force or the threat of it, whereas bargaining with North Korea continues, and Iran proceeds with its nuclear program. Developing and unstable countries from the world's "zone of war," which are most at odds with the existing international order, are the most eager to develop nuclear weapons to secure their regimes from outside intervention while continuing their own internal and external activities with impunity. These are precisely the countries the NPT most sought to stop.

A few scholars have argued that the spread of nuclear weapons would actually be a good thing, because it would expand to other regions of the world the same deterrence against war that prevailed between the blocs during the Cold War. Proponents of that approach dismiss any suggestion of differences in political behavior between developed and undeveloped or developing countries, and argue that the logic of mutual assured nuclear destruction is so compelling that even the most militant and unstable state authorities in the world's less developed areas are unlikely to initiate the use of nuclear weapons. Nor, they argue, are these states likely to compromise their control and hand over such weapons to terrorists. However, critics of this view doubt that the logic of MAD is foolproof, as nuclear weapons spread into a growing number of hands in less and less stable parts of the world. Such proliferation could, indeed, result in fewer wars, owing to nuclear deterrence, but it could also result in the eventual use of nuclear weapons—somewhere. Furthermore, critics point out that because the technological and institutional infrastructures are inferior in undeveloped countries, they are where the risk is greatest for an accidental use of nuclear weapons, or for a nuclear accident.[10]

With respect to terrorists, the greatest threat of nuclear proliferation—greater even than the prospect of nuclear weapons handed over to them by nuclear states—is the increased danger of leakage. Not only, as in the Pakistani case, may people and organizations with access to nuclear facilities sell or otherwise transfer nuclear materials, expertise, and even weapons to terrorists, with greater or lesser awareness by weak and segmented states; states in the less developed and unstable parts of the world are also in danger of disintegration and anarchy, which all but disappeared in the developed world. Again, Pakistan is a case in point, where the recent threat of a Taliban takeover, or a general anarchy, has been the cause of much alarm. When state authority collapses and anarchy takes hold, who will guarantee the security of a country's nuclear arsenal? The immense risks posed by the disintegration of the Soviet Union, with its nuclear and other non-conventional arsenal, may be the pattern of things to come if nuclear proliferation is allowed to go on unabated. The collapsed Soviet Union rather than the former nuclear superpower may be the model for future threats. The point is that nuclear proliferation is unlikely to stop at the state level and hence the logic of MAD is no guarantee of nuclear peace. This is reason enough to oppose nuclear proliferation.

Liberalism has been ambivalent about the sanctity of sovereignty. Sovereignty stands in the way of humanitarian intervention to enforce liberal rights abroad. On the other hand, forceful foreign intervention conflicts with the affluent liberal aversion to war that has only increased with time, particularly when such intervention has concerned matters of little direct impact on the vital national security interests of liberal powers, as in humanitarian intervention, and has proved increasingly messy. How does the potential for disaster foreshadowed by September 11 alter this traditional balance and affect affluent liberal democracies' policies? This question is the subject of a heated debate in the liberal democracies, polarizing attitudes within the United States and between the United States and Europe, to say nothing of reactions in the rest of the world. Each position within the intra-liberal argument is fraught with problems that partisan opponents are quick to point out.

The characteristically European claim that the continent's experience since 1945—peaceful cooperation through supra-national institutions—should be applied globally is beside the point. The Europe that emerged in the wake of World War II became possible by massive force and a crushing victory that imposed liberal democracy on the continent's previously nondemocratic and nonliberal countries. Liberal democracy, itself created through war, is what made Europe, and the West in general, into a Kantian world. Yet it is precisely the lack of such preconditions for a Kantian world that is the issue with respect to the non-liberal democratic and non-affluent parts of the world, where the frame is predominantly Hobbesian.[11] True, the success of the European experiment and the benefits of membership in the European Union enticed dictatorial countries of Southern Europe, and later the post-communist countries of Eastern Europe, to adopt liberal democracy in order to qualify for admission. Yet, though often proclaimed an "ideal," Europe is a geographical entity and cultural community, whose further expansion is therefore limited. And again, while the extension of economic benefits has been both the liberal ideal and the favored technique since the nineteenth century, it is precisely the countries and cultures that are unwilling or unable to be assimilated into the liberal orbit, and that react militantly, that are the concern. International institutions not based on a voluntary liberal consensus among affluent democracies are unlikely to have a better record than the League of Nations and the United Nations have had, for the reasons touched upon by Rousseau in his critique of Saint-Pierre (and elaborated in chapter 6, page122).

Appeasing potential sources of threat by offering them rewards and downright bribes to entice them to give up their development of WMD, particularly nuclear weapons, has much to recommend it, if and where it can be made to work. In the most difficult cases, however, it often cannot work, especially without the threat of force. Economic pressure and sanctions often seem promising in principle, but they have had a poor record since the 1930s. This is because the difficulties of binding all the major international players to effective sanctions frustrate the democracies, which are apprehensive about losing business to others. Containment is the main strategy against nuclear states, but is of very limited applicability in preventing states from *becoming* nuclear because it is not sufficient to isolate prospective developers of WMD within the confines of their own realm. The problem is development within that realm, the possible export or leakage of nuclear technology to others, and the chain reaction of further proliferation that such development may unleash in neighboring countries.

Thus the capability and willingness to use force, albeit as a last resort, appear to be indispensable for preventing WMD proliferation. This is a contentious issue within the liberal democracies, one that highlighted differences between the United States and Europe, especially during the presidency of George W. Bush. Those sympathetic to the Bush administration blamed European attitudes on a combination of naïve false consciousness, military impotence, and selfish free-riding on the only power that provides the essential public service of promoting global security. In this view, European societies are hedonistic, aging, and decadent, living in a fools' paradise made safe since World War II by American power, and hoping that the dangers from outside can be shut out. They fail even to live up to their own professed ideals and intervene by force to stop genocide, as in Rwanda (1994) and Sudan (2004). Only the American involvement that shouldered the burden finally made possible military intervention to stop ethnic cleansing in Europe's own backyard, in Bosnia (1995) and Kosovo (1999).[12] As none other than French President Nicolas Sarkozy put it: "Does Europe want to be left in peace or does Europe want peace?

We know what becomes of continents and countries whose sole ambition is to be left in peace: one day, they see the return of war."[13]

Certainly the policies associated with the post-9/11 United States—armed intervention to impose non-proliferation, active suppression of terror, and democracy as a means for the first two—involve their own intractable problems. As we have seen, democracy is neither desired by all nor unconditionally sustainable. In those parts of the world where conditions are less than auspicious, democratization should be seen as a complex and gradual process, to be pursued with discretion. There, the people's choice is often not liberalism or democracy, let alone moderation and peacefulness. And if the population is not waiting to be liberated, as is often assumed, then forceful intervention—which is sometimes unavoidable—becomes a far less attractive proposition, and may result in a political backlash and a military quagmire.

Defensive measures pose no less intricate problems. Like all other elements of the fight against terror, the disproportion between the terrorist investment and that required for states to mount a defense is enormous. As a result, a few critics have come close to suggesting that the United States should drop its expensive countermeasures and take its chances with the prospect of a biological or nuclear terror attack—a prospect they consider to be remote.* Between 2001 and 2008, the United States spent $57 billion on

---

* John Mueller, *Overblown: How Politicians and the Terrorism Industry Inflate National Security Threats and Why We Believe Them* (New York: Free Press, 2006), is a provocative corrective to the threat perception, emphasizing the difficulties of generating unconventional terror, the small number of casualties so far compared to other sources of mortality, and the counter-effectiveness of many of the measures employed. But it is spoiled by the author's one-sided depreciation of the threat and his bizarre suggestions that the U.S.'s involvement in World War II and the Cold War were equally unnecessary: the U.S. should not have gone to war after Pearl Harbor but merely stuck to economic sanctions and containment that would have brought down Japan (how, after the latter had conquered East Asia, thereby becoming self-sufficient, is unclear); nor should it have opposed Soviet expansion, because the failed Soviet system was in any case doomed.

bioterrorism defenses alone, including developing and stocking drugs, preparing hospitals, and surrounding 35 major cities with detection stations. And this is still judged to be insufficient in view of the increasing threat.[14]

The normative-legal aspects of the democracies' defensive measures are just as problematic. The expansion of the state's authority in such spheres as the detention of suspects by means of extraordinary legal procedures, debriefing methods, surveillance of people and communication, and other infringements of privacy, are hotly debated and litigated in the liberal democracies. As with the debate over foreign policy options, this legal-public debate assumes a bitterly ideological and righteous character. Indeed, all the measures concerned are deeply problematic for advanced liberal democratic societies. And yet the threat is real, will not go away anytime soon, and has no easy solutions. As encapsulated technologies of mass destruction proliferate and become available to non-state organizations and individuals, the prospect of their use seems to be a matter of "when" rather than "if." This is how William Cohen, American Defense Secretary under Clinton, put it even before September 11. Despite his sharp criticism of President George W. Bush's policies during his election campaign, President Barak Obama has expressed after his election a similar concern. It is the challenge of our times to contend with and adjust to the prospect of a "new world disorder" without losing the fundamental values that democratic societies live for and fight to keep.

Some readers may be surprised that I have treated all the above as tensions between conflicting strands within liberalism, since the controversy is more commonly presented as existing between liberals and (neo-)conservatives. Yet it is a measure of the remarkable march of liberalism and democracy since the eighteenth century that the liberal perspective has grown to completely dominate the public arena in the democracies. So-called conservatives in the liberal democracies have long embraced the classical liberal creed; indeed, they claim to be the true defenders of liberal tenets. Like all creeds, liberalism is susceptible to dogma that in pursuing the abstract fails to take heed of the realities with which abstract principles must connect. All the same, pragmatists and messianics of various persuasions, left and right, debate within the framework of liberalism, which is woven into the fabric of today's affluent democracies.

10
Conclusion: Strengths and Vulnerabilities

Liberal democracy's record of success derives from tremendous inner sources of strength, in both peace and war. Nonetheless, recent analysis of this record by scholars and public intellectuals has overrated structural factors and underrated historical contingency. Most notably, if it were not for the existence and exceptional continental size of the United States, the democracies would probably have lost both of the two World Wars to their capitalist nondemocratic rivals. A more context-sensitive understanding of the past ought to inspire greater humility. It should also inspire a sense of awe, not only at the underlying trends of the historical drama but also at its frailty and unfulfilled potentials, at the tremendous arbitrary forces and elements of chance that affect it. Deep structural factors and contingency both play their role in shaping even the most fateful of historical outcomes.

A more nuanced and realistic understanding of the past should also make us less complacent about the future. Currently, capitalist liberal democracies command among them more than three-fourths of the world's economic-military power, according to my estimates,[1] and their model exercises a global hegemony. But liberal democracy's future triumph is not preordained. With the return of the capitalist nondemocratic great powers, above all China, mighty challengers loom. As great-power conflict again becomes a possibility, a dispassionate comprehensive assessment of the strengths and weaknesses of liberal democracies' conflict behavior is needed. As scholars have begun to sense but have not yet fully laid out, liberal democracies exhibit a characteristic conflict behavior that grows ever more pronounced the more liberal, democratic, and economically developed they become.

Liberal democracies have been aptly labeled "powerful pacifists,"[2] and both of these terms require scrutiny. There are two main reasons for the liberal democracies' great power: they tend to be economically developed and wealthy; and they are politically inclusive. Liberalism and democracy correlated closely with capitalism, industrial-technological advance, and their social corollaries—each facilitating the other in a reciprocal causal relationship. Economic power, in turn, correlated very closely with military power and success in the great wars of the industrial age. Furthermore, inclusive political participation on a country scale was itself a function of economic development, urbanism, and the growth of "mass society." This fostered national integration, and increased people's stake in the state, strengthened the legitimacy of the state's political action, and enhanced social mobilization in support of it.

It should be remembered, however, that these sources of strength have not belonged exclusively to the democracies. Whereas communism proved to be an economic failure, nondemocratic capitalism was as successful economically as the democratic variant. In addition, both left- and right-wing authoritarian and totalitarian powers galvanized the masses through nondemocratic but comprehensive popular creeds. This, in conjunction with state terror (in the totalitarian cases), generated social commitment, mobilization levels, and tenacity that were at least as great as, if not greater than, those of the democracies.

Furthermore, the liberal democracies' sources of power are not undiluted. Historically, wealth and comfort tended to work against martial virtues. And although the positive relationship between wealth and power has become far stronger with modernity, the countervailing effect has not disappeared. Admittedly, this effect is likely to be felt in nondemocratic states as well, once they grow in wealth, but it seems to be stronger in societies where an individualistic rather than a more group-centered ethos prevails. Indeed, democratic inclusion in liberal societies that emphasize individual freedom and the pursuit of happiness also tends to weaken commitment to the sacrifice and self-sacrifice of life for remote collective ends.

This brings us from power to pacifism. Contrary to the precepts of the realist school of international relations, modern, economically advanced liberal democracies are unique in their international behavior, and this represents a historical change that is nothing less than revolutionary. All the developed countries of the industrial-technological era, including both capitalist and non-capitalist (e.g., communist) countries, have been far more powerful but less belligerent than premodern states. Yet liberal and democratic societies have been inherently more attuned to modernity's pacifying aspects. Relying on arbitrary coercive force at home, nonliberal and nondemocratic countries have found it more natural to use force abroad. By contrast, in liberal democracies, war remains legitimate only under narrow and narrowing formal and practical conditions, and is generally viewed as abhorrent.

The fruits of these deepening trends are little short of amazing. Their most striking and widely-noted manifestation is the inter-democratic peace. With growing liberalization, democracy, and economic development (all interrelated), the probability of war between democracies declines to a vanishing point. The liberal democracies' aversion to war is multiplied several times over in their relations among themselves. A positive peace, based on shared interests, outlook, and ideals, rather than on the balance of power and deterrence, prevails. Thus the wealthiest and actually or potentially most powerful regions on earth constitute zones of peace. There has been nothing like this in world history, as neighboring great powers always fought each other in the greatest of wars. Domestically too, on account of their stronger consensual nature, plurality, tolerance, and, indeed, the greater legitimacy of peaceful secession, advanced liberal democracies have become practically free from civil war, the most lethal and destructive type of war. An economically developed liberal democratic world, if it ever materializes, promises to be peaceful.

Yet not all regions of the world are economically developed, and among states that will develop economically, not all may turn out to be liberal democracies. Democracies' relationships with developed nondemocratic powers are increasingly less likely to involve full-scale war, both because of nuclear deterrence and because these countries share the reduced belligerency of the developed world, especially if the global system remains economically open. This reflects the impact of economic development and open trade, but not the inter-democratic cause of peace. Under these conditions, mutual suspicion, insecurity, and arms races of varying intensity are likely to continue. Heightened tensions, conflicts, Cold War situations, and limited military escalations are possible and will have to be prepared for and endured.

What remains are the smaller wars, which may be accentuated by great power rivalries, but which have an independent existence. Democracies continue to be sporadically involved, as they have since 1945, in wars with little-developed nondemocratic rivals that are less affected by either of the pacifying trends above, and therefore also continue to fight among themselves. Such rivals, though, are constrained by their weakness, as their military forces and civilian infrastructure are vulnerable in war to crippling blows. However, by switching to irregular warfare and taking cover within a friendly civilian environment, they are able to frustrate if not deter invasion and occupation. They continue the fight by taking advantage of the liberal democracies' self-imposed limitations on ruthlessness against civilians. Fighting guerillas is widely assumed to be difficult, but in reality it is far more difficult for some than for others. In the quest to explain the differences in capability and attitude in wars between developed liberal democracies and little-developed rivals, it has been quipped that while the former are able to kill, the latter are still prepared to be killed. The truth, though, is that in addition to the democracies' much lower tolerance for accepting their own casualties, their tolerance for killing others is also greatly circumscribed.

As a result, the democracies end up with a paradoxically losing combination in many small wars: they sacrifice capability to humanitarian considerations but still face a heightened outcry both at home and abroad over the war's atrocities, the killing of civilians, and collateral damage. These by-products of war are regrettable and partly avoidable, but are often trifling by the standards of nondemocratic powers. As democracies are unable to win under such conditions, their mounting costs—above all casualties that may be historically and comparatively small—spur national trauma. Thus advanced liberal democracies' aversion to and inhibitions in war tend to make even small wars against weak rivals an unbearable mess for them, which, in turn, only magnifies their aversion.

There is a catch here that lies at the root of affluent liberal democracies' torment in conflict situations. Since liberal societies abhor wars as antithetical to their interests and values, to their entire way of life and worldview, they sanction wars only as a last resort, when all other options have failed. Yet there is virtually no situation in which it can be clear that all alternatives to war have been exhausted and that war has become unavoidable. The sense that there may be another way—that there *must* be another way—always lingers. Errors of omission or commission are always suspected as the cause of undesired belligerency. Moreover, the democracies never view themselves as coming to a conflict with entirely clean hands; prior wrongs are always alleged. Nor indeed can the democracies ever be morally pure, given the gap that inevitably separates ideals from reality.

The democracies' reaction to the Axis challenge during the 1930s epitomizes this predicament. They did everything they could to avoid military action, let alone a disastrous slide into war, even if it meant allowing Germany to regain power, grow in confidence, and cross the point of no return on its road to expansion. The democracies' bad conscience for not having treated Germany in good faith after World War I contributed to their paralysis. As long as the prospect of peaceful accommodation and containment remained— and it hardly ever faded, not even in 1939—they would not initiate armed confrontation. More or less the same spirit animated their reaction to the challenges that Japan and Italy posed. To be sure, as critics caution, Hitlers are rare and not every crisis is the 1930s. All the same, the 1930s are a standing reminder that the democracies' strong aversion to war, while immensely beneficial overall, can be a grave problem in serious conflict situations.

It is often said that the democracies' inhibitions and self-imposed constraints are a source of moral strength that when all else fails and war erupts, galvanizes their resolve and helps them gain the upper hand. Although there is some truth to this, it is more than a touch idealized, resting largely on heroic images from World War II. In reality, if anything, the Axis powers fought more tenaciously than the democracies, and it was the United States' superior size and strength (in combination with that of the Soviet Union) that proved decisive, rescuing the democracies from their initial grave blunders and severe setbacks. Moreover, since World War II, the democracies' pacification has increased significantly as a result of growing liberalism and affluence, the transformation of societies from physical, farm- and factory-based labor to metropolitan-service occupations, and the rise of postmodern values.

This book should not be interpreted as a moral and political critique of liberal democracy, or as a call for change. I am not arguing that liberal democracies' attitude toward and conduct in war can or should be fundamentally altered. On the contrary, I believe both are deeply structural and thoroughly imbedded in the democracies' makeup and outlook—written in their DNA, so to speak. They correspond to the general parameters within which liberal society thinks and works. Those parameters can be challenged but not radically altered. Thus, for better or worse, the democracies have their characteristic way in conflict, with its strengths and vulnerabilities. Of course, there still remains a significant range of conduct among the democracies, depending on circumstances of all sorts, and there is much that can be done to improve policy and strategy within that range. A better awareness of the underlying patterns of the democracies' behavior in conflict, both *ad bellum* and *in bello*, might help. To that end, and in view of the ongoing unpredictability of what can and will occur in the world, the following is a rough sketch intended to illustrate some trends and potentials.

Given their fundamental view of conflict and war as harmful and deeply contradictory to their experience of the good life, hopes for mutually-rewarding international cooperation and peaceful accommodation, humanitarian universalism, and sense of guilt—the liberal democracies are likely to find a revival of great-power conflicts agonizing. In forming policy in such circumstances, they are once again likely to vacillate between isolationism, appeasement, containment, and Cold War—progressing most reluctantly up this ladder, and down whenever deemed possible. In military confrontations with smaller rivals, the democracies will tend to prefer war by proxy, blockade, naval and aerial actions, and limited operations by technologically superior strike forces. Because of far-away global commitments, and the unwillingness of citizens to enlist for military service, the democracies are likely to continue their shift towards employing professional forces. Still, ever-growing sensitivity decreases liberal democracies' tolerance of casualties among professional troops as well.

Legal and normative constraints on the conduct of war, or "lawfare," are gaining potency in liberal societies and their international institutional offshoots. An older view of war as a clash between national collectives, mobilized societies, and conflicting communal wills is increasingly giving way to a view of the enemy population as disassociated from its political leadership. The enemy so understood is held to possess a right of immunity from collective pressure, often interpreted to cover not only life but also disruption of civilian well-being and destruction of dual-function civilian-strategic infrastructure.* A demand for a greater reliance on non-lethal weapons, even against combatants, may lie ahead. The democracies are torn by arguments regarding the effectiveness and legitimacy of means—both at home and abroad—to counter the threats posed by nuclear proliferation, the biotechnological revolution, and unconventional terror. If such terror strikes, the line of legitimacy could move substantially. All the same, liberal democracies are much more vulnerable to terror, including unconventional terror, than are strong authoritarian and totalitarian countries.

There are variations, of course, within and among the democracies. Europe is the most pacific, for a number of reasons. The continent's ruin in two World Wars deeply affected its liberal societies, none more than devastated and reformed Germany, Europe's most

---

* A full acceptance of such a doctrine wholly negates nuclear deterrence, which rests on the proposition that the enemy's civilian population is held hostage to a credible threat of annihilation in case of a nuclear attack on one's own civilian population. There is no known defense against a wholesale nuclear attack other than deterrence through mutual assured destruction. Of course, such credible deterrence actually decreases the prospect of a nuclear annihilation. For an intelligent discussion of the irreconcilable moral dilemmas here, see Michael Walzer, *Just and Unjust War* (New York: Basic Books, 1977), chap. 17.

powerful country. The European Union, far from being a mega-state, is a collective of medium- and small-sized countries that retain their separate national and political identities. They are too small to act on the global scene independently, while the Union framework commands neither military forces nor legitimacy to send soldiers into action. Partly for this reason, Europe's reliance on the United States for its defense after World War II became a habit of considerable cultural significance. By the 1970s, the countries of Western Europe had grown about three times as rich as the Soviet Union, and potentially that much more powerful, ranking close to the United States.[3] Only its unwillingness to match American military spending (not to mention that of the USSR) prevented Europe from developing the capability to withstand the Soviet challenge on its own. Since then, Europe has greatly expanded its territory and increased its wealth, but the overall picture remains the same. Indeed, capabilities and attitudes are closely connected, as Europeans have grown accustomed to regarding their successful experience of peaceful integration, sheltered under the American military umbrella, as a universal political and moral model. With the collapse of the Soviet Union and the Soviet bloc, any sense among Europeans of a concrete military danger on their doorstep has evaporated. Hence European attitudes combine strong pacifist tendencies, the perception that no acute foreign threat exists, and disdain for American power politics, on the one hand, with concern that the United States will become weak and withdraw from its role as the guarantor of the global order, on the other. With reality shaping consciousness, the United States and Europe traded orientations during the twentieth century, the former becoming less withdrawn and less pacifist and the latter more so—with rhetoric to match.

Moreover, many Europeans do not view their main threat as military. Radicalization among Europe's Islamic communities is breeding terror. But the civilian aspect of that radicalization is at least as alarming: the prospect of Islamic intolerance, deeply alien to Western values and the liberal creed, taking hold in communities that are fast expanding through high birth rates and immigration. The only liberal remedy to this challenge is successful assimilation of these communities into the European countries' liberal framework, which in reality also means the various national cultures. In addition, stiffening immigration laws, attempts to enact mandatory codes of conduct in the public sphere, and growing opposition to the admission of Turkey into the European Union signal a retreat from cherished European beliefs after 1945 that nation and culture do not matter. If all these means fail, Europe's liberal democracies may come under pressure from the far right as well as from radical Islam.

Liberal democratic Japan is in some ways similar to and in some ways different from Europe. Like Germany, Japan was devastated by World War II, and thoroughly reformed in its wake. But unlike many European countries, Japan neither opened its gates to foreign immigration nor embraced multiculturalism. As a result, it is among the world's most homogeneous countries. With pacifism and low military expenditure enshrined in its constitution, Japan relied on the United States for security during the Cold War. Unlike Europe, however, Japan has been witnessing the growth of a new mega-threat—China—in its close vicinity. While the two countries are economically interdependent, Japan is deeply concerned about Chinese power and hostility, and looks to the United States for leadership and support.

India is the greatest unknown. There is nothing quite like it. It is still a poor country, about twice as poor today as China, and like China, possesses a vast population. And yet it is a well-established democracy. Having adopted capitalism, and having benefited tremendously from globalization, India is experiencing rapid economic growth, albeit not as rapid as that of nondemocratic China. Indian democracy will be facing the need to accommodate the pressures of development. Even more challenging may be the pressures on India's unified national identity, which may arise in this ethnically heterogeneous democracy that is undergoing modernization and urbanization. It remains to be seen how tensions with Pakistan (another nuclear country), threats of terror and of separatist secession, proximity to China, and unique culture will come together to shape India's conduct in conflict situations.

As we have seen, the United States was the single most important factor in the triumph of democracy during the twentieth century. The U.S.—capitalist, developed, and large—held close to one-third of the world's wealth and power throughout the twentieth century, and was always stronger than the second- and third- greatest powers combined. The question of America's power and its role in the twenty-first century is obviously of crucial significance. As Fareed Zakaria has observed, America's relative share of the world's wealth and power are bound to erode as other countries previously averse to capitalism successfully embrace it. However, the United States' capacity for absorbing immigrants remains an incomparable engine of superior growth and substantially limits that erosion. The main change in the twenty-first century will not be America's overall share of world power as much as its share and ranking relative to other powers no longer either undeveloped or smaller. Given China's current low levels of development, it still has a very long way to go before it catches up with the United States, not merely in GDP, but in GDP per capita, a critical measure of development, wealth, and power. All the same, with its successful embrace of the market, rapid development, and huge size, China may close the gap and possibly even overtake the United States by the second half of the century.

There is another factor too. During the Cold War, the democracies' military spending as a share of their total GDP was much lower than that of the Soviet Union, averaging 5-6 percent for the United States and 3-4 percent for the West European countries, as opposed to around 12 percent for the USSR (recent assessments suggest that Soviet military expenditure was perhaps even double). That was more than sufficient to meet the challenge, given the Soviet Union's economic backwardness, which forced the Soviets to struggle much harder to keep up militarily. Indeed, the Soviet Union's higher relative military spending increased the strain on an already badly-functioning economy and contributed to the system's collapse. But Cold War patterns and habits of mind may no longer hold. Careful not to choke its staggering economic takeoff, China spent only 2.5 percent of its GDP on its military during the 1990s. Over the past decade, however, its military spending has increased by a double-digit percentage every year. As a share of GDP, it is estimated to have grown higher than U.S.'s current rate of around 4 percent. Because the United States is far wealthier than China, its absolute military spending is many times greater. But as China's GDP grows, and assuming it retains or further increases its level of military spending, China may overtake the United States in military spending even before the economic gap between the two closes. There is no reason to suppose that China would replicate the Soviet Union's levels of military spending, or its Cold War hostility. Yet a high-performance capitalist economy, coupled with a higher priority for military spending than exists in the democracies, may pose a challenge for the democracies unlike any since 1945. This challenge may also increase the strains over burden-sharing among the United States, Europe, Japan, and possibly India. It is a cliché, but true nonetheless, that the United States will need to find common interest and work with its allies.

The global economic crisis that broke out in 2007-2008 casts a new shadow on the reputation of both the United States and liberal democracy itself. Analogies with the 1930s are inevitable. Having been the world's only superpower and the widely envied model of success during the 1920s, the United States suffered a crushing blow with the Great Depression, turned inward, and left the scene to fascist and communist totalitarianism, which throve on the apparent failure of capitalist democracy. There is reason to believe that the current economic crisis and its repercussions will not be nearly as catastrophic. Capitalism will be adjusted and amended both domestically and internationally. The United States will need serious domestic reconstruction, including kicking its recent habit of living beyond its means. But it will remain the paramount power after the crisis, as it did in the 1930s, while avoiding isolationism. Hopefully, the world will also resist protectionist pressures. All the same, the global allure of state-driven and nationalist capitalist authoritarianism may grow.

I intend no scaremongering. The liberal democracies are likely to remain prosperous and powerful. Their model is mostly benevolent, enticing, and influential. Great-power conflict need not materialize, most of the time. Mutually-beneficial international economic relations may continue to prosper. The exercise of peaceful soft power from outside (backed by overwhelming wealth and power), coupled with indigenous domestic socio-economic development, remain the most potent agents of democratization, as they have since 1945. All these are grounded in powerful trends underlying modernization, but also in the existing geopolitical contours of today's world, shaped by its particular historical path. At the same time, there are contravening forces at work, both material and cultural. The future is less secure than it was deemed to be in the wake of the Cold War, and the triumph of democracy is not inevitable.

The great ideologies of the modern era have been described as secular religions. This label was first applied to Marxism and fascism, but, with some differences, it also applies to liberalism. Offering a comprehensive interpretation of the world, a creed of justice, and a quasi-sanctified code of conduct, liberalism involves great emotional investment and evokes much zeal (albeit not necessarily a strong commitment to action and willingness to sacrifice). Like other grand ideologies, it espouses a secularized sacred history, depicting a march toward ultimate triumph. That liberal democracy emerged victorious from the great-power struggles of the twentieth century is hugely encouraging. But this fact should not give rise to myth-making and complacency; it should not blind us to liberal democracy's weaknesses; and it should not make us lose touch with the challenges ahead. To advance the cause of liberal democracy, we must understand both the reasons for its victories and the sources of its vulnerabilities.

Democracies' Unique Traits in Conflict

The now widely recognized inter-democratic peace phenomenon should have suggested that liberal democracies' conflict behavior may be distinctive in other significant ways. Scholars have pointed out some of its unique traits, but others remain unnoted, and the lot has scarcely been tied together as a comprehensive whole. The following is a concise (though not exhaustive) list of major features of the liberal democracies' typical conflict behavior discussed in this book:

1. A positive peace prevails among liberal democracies, which no longer fear or prepare for the possibility of conflict with one another. This deepening trend increases with growing liberalism and democracy, as well as with economic development, affluence, and interdependence—all of which partly correlate with liberal democracy.

2. Liberal democracies have been less prone to war than nondemocracies by various measurements. First, they have fought fewer interstate wars than nondemocracies during the past two centuries, partly because of the scarcity of war between democracies. Second, the wars they have fought have been, on average, less severe than those fought

by nondemocracies in terms of their own casualties. This is partly because the democracies have tended to be technologically and economically superior to, and therefore more powerful than, most non-democracies.

3. Controlling for both economic development and the balance of power, liberal democracies do not appear to win wars more often than nondemocracies. Historically, economically developed, capitalist nondemocratic powers simply happened to be smaller than the democracies (namely, the U.S.), so their defeats were due to size, not regime type.

4. Liberal democracies are inclined to favor the status quo and to adopt strategies that avoid war. They typically eschew preventive wars, and their strategic policy usually progresses up a scale beginning with isolationism and moving to appeasement, containment and Cold War, limited war, and only lastly to full-scale war. This applies mainly to their conflicts with strong nondemocratic powers, but increasingly also to their conflicts with much weaker rivals.

5. Liberal democracies are highly sensitive to casualties in conflict, and this sensitivity grows more acute the more liberal, democratic, affluent, and interdependent they become. This sensitivity is greater the less existential and less necessary a war is perceived to be, but liberal democracies increasingly tend to view *all* wars as unnecessary. The sensitivity is also greater the smaller the prospects of success, but liberal democracies' ability to achieve victory is sharply diminished in some types of wars by their characteristic conduct as liberal democracies.

6. Liberal democracies are particularly ineffective in counterinsurgency wars, in which their growing, self-imposed limitations on violence against civilians—especially marked in wars against weak rivals and in non-desperate situations—prevent them from using the crushing suppression typical of imperial rule. Thus liberal democracies often lose against vastly weaker rivals, irrespective of the balance of power between the sides.

7. Liberal democracies have been more extensively involved than nondemocracies in wars with non-state actors, especially insurgents, during the past two centuries. This record may be misleading, however, for two main reasons. First, liberal democratic powers were saddled with colonial empires, which other, nondemocratic powers were late to acquire and lost early, in the World Wars. Second, as they have become more liberal, the democracies have increasingly proved ineffective at forceful suppression, whereas totalitarian and strong authoritarian states have successfully threatened and employed ruthless means to deter insurgencies or nip them in the bud.

8. Developed liberal democracies tend not to experience civil wars because of their consensual nature and the greater legitimacy they grant to peaceful secession. Civil wars mainly afflict less developed democracies and weak nondemocracies. Totalitarian and strong authoritarian states also have little experience with civil wars, but this record is again deceptive because they prevent such wars through harsh suppression.

9. Liberal democracies are far more vulnerable to terror (including future unconventional terror) than are totalitarian and strong authoritarian countries. This is due to liberal democracies' open society, their weaker surveillance, policing, and suppression capabilities, and their media's far greater resonance.

Notes

1

1. The idea goes back to the nineteenth century, but the modern argument was seminally made by Seymour Lipset in his *Political Man* (New York: Anchor, 1963). More recently see Francis Fukuyama, *The End of History and the Last Man* (New York: Free Press, 1992); Michael Mandelbaum, *The Ideas that Conquered the World: Peace, Democracy, and Free Markets in the Twenty-First Century* (New York: Public Affairs, 2002); Mandelbaum, *Democracy's Good Name: The Rise and Risks of the World's Most Popular Form of Government* (New York: Public Affairs, 2007).

2. The democratic success in war attracted considerable attention in the study of international relations and is the subject of Dan Reiter and Allan Stam, *Democracies at War* (Princeton, N.J.: Princeton University Press, 2002). I agree with some of this book's conclusions, *inter alia* that alliances were not the reason for the success, while differing with quite a few of its other conclusions, as seen below. More on alliance choices: Randolph Siverson and Julian Emmons, "Birds of a Feather: Democratic Political Systems and Alliance Choices," *Journal of Conflict Resolution* 35 (1991): 285-306; Michael Simon and Erik Gartzke, "Political System Similarity and the Choice of Allies," *Journal of Conflict Resolution* 40 (1996): 617-35. For a summary of the literature see Bruce Russett and John Oneal, *Triangulating Peace: Democracy, Interdependence, and International Organizations* (New York: Norton, 2001), pp. 59-60, 66-68.

3. For example, Richard Overy, *Why the Allies Won* (New York: Norton, 1996), chap. 9. Although otherwise highly statistical in nature, Reiter and Stam's *Democracies at War* concludes without providing any evidence that democracies proved superior in war largely because democratic troops were better motivated and therefore fought better than their rivals. At least with respect to the World Wars—by far the most crucial for the fate of democracy—this

conclusion finds little support in reality. For other criticisms see: Michael Desch, "Democracies and Victory: Why Regime Type Hardly Matters," *International Security* 27.2 (2002): 5-47. For the main oversight, in my opinion, see note 7 below.

4. Overy, *Why the Allies Won*, chaps. 1, 6-7; also, Randall Schweller, *Deadly Imbalances: Tripolarity and Hitler's Strategy of World Conquest* (New York: Columbia University Press, 1998).

5. Niall Ferguson, *The Cash Nexus: Money and Power in the Modern World, 1700-2000* (New York: Basic Books, 2001), p. 404. For the data: Overy, *Why the Allies Won*, pp. 42-43, 46-48; Mark Harrison in Mark Harrison, ed., *The Economies of World War II: Six Great Powers in International Comparison* (Cambridge, Eng.: Cambridge University Press, 1998), pp. 20-21, 47, 82-83, 88-89, 157-59, 257, 287. The high mobilization rates of modern authoritarian/totalitarian regimes have also been noted by Michael Mann in his *The Sources of Social Power, Vol. 2: The Rise of Classes and Nation-States, 1760-1914* (Cambridge, Eng.: Cambridge University Press, 1993), p. 60.

6. Mandelbaum, *The Ideas that Conquered the World*, pp. 79-86; Mandelbaum, *Democracy's Good Name*, p. 71. Fukuyama, *The End of History*, pp. 16-17, 127-29, may be more aware of the ambivalence of the outcome, but is equally cursory.

7. For example, this factor is not mentioned in Robert Dahl, *On Democracy* (New Haven, Conn.: Yale University Press, 1998), pp. 163-65; though his *Polyarchy* (New Haven, Conn.: Yale University Press, 1971) does recognize foreign occupation and influence as a possible cause of democracy. Nor is the U.S. factor mentioned in Ferguson, *The Cash Nexus*, chap. 12, despite the chapter's title: "The American Wave: Democracy's Flow and Ebb." Also, implicitly, Michael Doyle, *Ways of War and Peace: Realism, Liberalism, and Socialism* (New York: Norton, 1997), pp. 269-70, 277. Above all see Mandelbaum, *The Ideas that Conquered the World*, pp. 87-95; Mandelbaum, *Democracy's Good Name*, beginning on p. 66; and Walter Russell Mead, *God and Gold: Britain, America, and the Making of the Modern World* (New York: Knopf, 2007), which is very good on the unique sources of British and American power but has little to say about the twentieth century. Fukuyama, in *The End of History*, pp. 16-17, 127-29, writes that fascism was defeated because it clashed with the international system, but he fails to mention the reason why that "system" was stronger; after all, there were two opposing coalitions. Reiter and Stam, in *Democracies at War*, p. 136, recognize that it was the United States' participation that tilted the scales in both Europe and the Pacific, but reject this as an explanation for the democracies' military success with the comment that one should not generalize from a single case; apparently not even if this case involves by far the greatest global power, whose participation decided the twentieth century's

mightiest military conflicts and the fate of democracy. Samuel Huntington, in *The Third Wave: Democratization in the Late Twentieth Century* (Norman: University of Oklahoma, 1991), is well aware of the international context, including the victories in the two World Wars, though he does not discuss the reasons for the democracies' victories in these wars. And see Tony Smith, *America's Mission: The United States and the Worldwide Struggle for Democracy in the Twentieth Century* (Princeton, N.J.: Princeton University Press, 1994), pp. 10-12, 147.

8. Daniel Deudney and G. John Ikenberry, "The Myth of Autocratic Revival," *Foreign Affairs*, 88.1 (2009).

9. Robert Barro, "Determinants of Economic Growth: A Cross-Country Empirical Study," *National Bureau of Economic Research Working Paper*, 5698 (1996); Amartya Sen, *Development and Freedom* (New York: Knopf, 1999), which offers little historical perspective. Theoretically, see Mancur Olson, *Power and Prosperity: Outgrowing Communist and Capitalist Dictatorships* (New York: Basic Books, 2000). Ferguson, *The Cash Nexus*, pp. 348-49, 363-69, is a good summary and analysis; also, Fukuyama, *The End of History*, p. 123. Two comprehensive studies—Adam Przeworski, Michael Alvarez, Jose Cheibub, and Fernando Limongi, *Democracy and Development* (Cambridge, Eng.: Cambridge University Press, 2000), which is excellent, and the more limited book by Morton Halperin, Josef Siegle, and Michael Weinstein, *The Democracy Advantage: How Democracies Promote Prosperity and Peace* (New York: Routledge, 2005)—both fail to distinguish between capitalist and non-capitalist (including communist!) dictatorships and to account for the staggering performance of the East Asian capitalist nondemocratic economies.

10. Huntington, *The Third Wave*.

11. For a summary of references to the earlier belief in inevitable democratization, see Kellee Tsai, *Capitalism without Democracy* (Ithaca, N.Y.: Cornell University Press, 2007), pp. 2-3, 5; Mandelbaum, *Democracy's Good Name*, p. 206. John Gray offered a general antithesis to the prevailing trend in his *False Dawn: The Delusions of Global Capitalism* (London: Granta, 1998); and for a focus on China see: Tsai, *Capitalism without Democracy*; David Shambaugh, *China's Communist Party: Atrophy and Adaptation* (Berkeley: University of California Press, 2008); James Mann, *The China Fantasy: Why Capitalism Will Not Bring Democracy to China* (New York: Penguin, 2008); Mark Leonard, *What Does China Think?* (London: Fourth Estate, 2008).

2

1. More recently, see: E. L. Jones, *The European Miracle: Environments, Economies, and Geopolitics in the History of Europe and Asia* (Cambridge, Eng.: Cambridge University Press, 1987); John Hall, *Power and Liberties: The*

Causes and Consequences of the Rise of the West (Oxford: Basil Blackwell, 1985); David Landes, *The Wealth and Poverty of Nations* (New York: Norton, 1999).

2. Montesquieu, *The Spirit of the Laws* (Cambridge, Eng.: Cambridge University Press, 1989), 17:6; also 17:4. A rare treatment of these questions is offered in Jared Diamond's Epilogue to his *Guns, Germs, and Steel: The Fate of Human Societies* (New York: Norton, 1997), pp. 411-16; also, in Jones's footsteps, Fareed Zakaria, *The Future of Freedom: Illiberal Democracy at Home and Abroad* (New York: Norton, 2004), pp. 35-38.

3. Although the elaboration of this old idea by Karl Vittfogel in his *Oriental Despotism* (New Haven, Conn.: Yale University Press, 1967) has been rightly criticized on various grounds, it remains fundamentally valid. Cf. Moses I. Finley, *The Ancient Economy* (Berkeley: University of California Press, 1973), p. 31.

4. Although challenged by some recent scholarship, I believe this picture, which originated with Adam Smith and Karl Marx, remains broadly valid: Adam Smith, *The Wealth of Nations*, bk. IV, chap. vii; Karl Marx and Friedrich Engels, "Manifesto of the Communist Party"; Karl Marx, *The Capital* (London: Penguin, 1976), chap. 31; Fernand Braudel, *Civilization & Capitalism, 15th-18th Century, Volume 2: The Wheels of Commerce* (Berkeley: University of California Press, 1992), p. 601; Immanuel Wallerstein, *The Modern World System I: Capitalist Agriculture and the Origins of the European World-Economy in the Sixteenth Century* (New York: Academic Press, 1974); Andre Frank, *World Accumulation 1492-1789* (New York: Monthly Review, 1978). Recent research has rightly emphasized Europe's internal economic growth, but the two developments were obviously mutually-reinforcing. According to Patrick O'Brien, "European Economic Development: The Contribution of the Periphery," *Economic History Review*, 35 (1982): 1-18, Europe's global commercial activities constituted only 25 percent of its trade even as late as 1790. However, see Neils Steensgaard, "Commodities, Bullion and Services in Intercontinental Transactions before 1750," ibid., 9-23 (and the data compiled by Frank, 105-106, 215-19, 225, 232-33). As O'Brien himself acknowledges, it is often the marginal economic advantage that counts. Even Kenneth Pomeranz, *The Great Divergence: China, Europe, and the Making of the Modern World Economy* (Princeton, N.J.: Princeton University Press, 2000), concedes the crucial marginal advantage accorded by the Europeans' global position; also, Janet Abu-Lughod, *Before European Hegemony: The World System A.D. 1250-1350* (New York: Oxford University Press, 1989), p. 363. Finally, Angus Maddison, *The World Economy: A Millennial Perspective* (Paris: OECD, 2001), p. 93, shows that in the case of the leading British economy, extra-European trade was not marginal but constituted about half the country's overall trade by 1774.

5. Joseph Needham, Wang Ling, and Lu Gwei-Djen, *Science and Civilization in China, Volume 4, Part iii: Nautical Technology* (Cambridge, Eng.: Cambridge

University Press, 1971), pp. 379-99; Louise Levathes, *When China Ruled the Seas: The Treasure Fleet of the Dragon Throne 1405-1433* (New York: Oxford University Press, 1994).

6. J. H. Parry, *The Discovery of the Sea* (Berkeley: University of California Press, 1981); Bailey Diffie and George Winius, *Foundations of the Portuguese Empire, 1415-1580* (St Paul: University of Minnesota, 1977).

7. Smith, *The Wealth of Nations*, V.I.i.

8. Peter Mathias and Patrick O'Brien, "Taxation in England and France, 1715-1810. A Comparison of the Social and Economic Incidence of Taxes Collected for the Central Governments," *Journal of European Economic History*, 5 (1976): 601-50; Richard Bonney, "The Eighteenth Century. II. The Struggle for Great Power Status and the End of the Old Fiscal Regime," in his (ed.), *Economic Systems and State Finance, 13th to 18th Centuries* (Oxford: Oxford University Press, 1995), pp. 315-90.

9. John Brewer, *The Sinews of Power: War, Money and the English State, 1688-1783* (London: Unwin Hyman, 1989), pp. 180-83.

10. For the significance of property rights, see Douglas North and Robert Thomas, *The Rise of the Western World: A New Economic History* (Cambridge, Eng.: Cambridge University Press, 1973).

11. Tenney Frank, *An Economic Survey of Ancient Rome, I: Rome and Italy of the Republic* (Paterson, N.J.: Pageant, 1959), pp. 62, 75, 79-94.

12. Jean-Claude Hocquet, "City-State and Market Economy," in Bonney, *Economic Systems and State Finance*, pp. 87-100; Martin Körner, "Expenditure" and "Public Credit," ibid., pp. 403, 407, 413, 515, 523, and passim.

13. See Emmanuel le Roy Ladurie, *The Royal French State 1460-1610* (Oxford: Blackwell, 1994), pp. 17, 130, for the civil offices; and John Childs, *Armies and Warfare in Europe 1648-1789* (Manchester, Eng.: Manchester University Press, 1982), pp. 81-82, for the military.

14. Geoffrey Parker, "War and Economic Change: The Economic Costs of the Dutch Revolt," in J. Winter (ed.), *War and Economic Development* (Cambridge, Eng.: Cambridge University Press, 1975), p. 57.

15. Bonney, "Great Power Status," p. 345.

16. P. Dickson, *The Financial Revolution in England* (London: Macmillan, 1967), pp. 470-85, especially 470-71; Bonney, "Great Power Status," p. 345; Körner, "Public Credit," pp. 507-38; Geoffrey Parker, *The Army of Flanders*

and the Spanish Road 1567-1659 (Cambridge, Eng.: Cambridge University Press, 1972), p. 151; and on the long-term perspective, Raymond Goldsmith, *Premodern Financial Systems: A Historical Comparative Study* (Cambridge, Eng.: Cambridge University Press, 1987), pp. 26, 44, 139, and passim.

17. Dickson, *The Financial Revolution*, pp. 10, 304-37 (especially 320); Brewer, *The Sinews of Power*, pp. 30, 114-17; Niall Ferguson, *The Cash Nexus: Money and Power in the Modern World 1700-2000* (New York: Basic Books, 2001).

18. Perry Anderson, *Lineages of the Absolutist State* (London: NLB, 1974); Hillay Zmora, *Monarchy, Aristocracy and the State in Europe 1300-1800* (London: Routledge, 2001).

19. Mathias and O'Brien, "Taxation in England and France"; Brewer, *The Sinews of Power*, pp. 89-91, and passim; also Philip T. Hoffman and Kathryn Norberg (eds.), *Fiscal Crises, Liberty, and Representative Government, 1450-1789* (Stanford, Calif.: Stanford University Press, 1994); I. A. A. Thompson, "Castile: Polity, Fiscality, and Fiscal Crisis," ibid., p. 176; Phyllis Deane and W. Cole, *British Economic Growth 1688-1959* (Cambridge, Eng.: Cambridge University Press, 1967), pp. 2-3; Michael Mann, States, *War and Capitalism* (Oxford: Blackwell, 1988); Mann, *The Sources of Social Power, Volume 2: The Rise of Classes and Nation States, 1760-1914* (Cambridge, Eng.: Cambridge University Press), pp. 214-15, 369-70; Juan Gelabert, "The Fiscal Burden," in Bonney, *State Finance*, p. 560; and a useful summary of research in Thomas Ertman, *Birth of the Leviathan: Building States and Regimes in Medieval and Early Modern Europe* (Cambridge, Eng.: Cambridge University Press, 1997), p. 220. For the older view, see e.g. F. Gilbert (ed.), *The Historical Essays of Otto Hintze* (New York: Oxford University Press, 1975). Since the original publication of my text, two new excellent treatments of these themes have appeared: Walter Russell Mead, *God and Gold: Britain, America and the Making of the Modern World* (New York: Knopf, 2007), especially chap. 8; Ronald Findlay and Kevin O'Rourke, *Power and Plenty: Trade, War, and the World Economy in the Second Millennium* (Princeton, N.J.: Princeton University Press, 2007), chap. 5.

20. Joseph Strayer, *On the Medieval Origins of the Modern State* (Princeton, N.J.: Princeton University Press, 1970), pp. 11-12 and passim.

21. Bernard Lewis, *Cultures in Conflict: Christians, Muslims, and Jews in the Age of Discovery* (New York: Oxford University Press, 1995), p. 23.

22. See e.g. Joad Raymond, *The Invention of the Newspaper: English Newsbooks 1641-1649* (Oxford: Oxford University Press, 1996); Bob Harris, *Politics and the Rise of the Press: Britain and France, 1620-1800* (London: Routledge, 1996).

23. Smith, *The Wealth of Nations*, bk. III, chaps. ii and iv. This is picked up by Jones, *The European Miracle*, chap. 5. See also Mancur Olson, *Power and Prosperity: Outgrowing Communist and Capitalist Dictatorships* (New York: Basic Books, 2000), pp. 60-61.

24. For more on this, see Barrington Moore's classic *Social Origins of Dictatorship and Democracy: Lord and Peasant in the Making of the Modern World* (Boston: Beacon, 1966), chap. 1.

25. For a quantitative analysis see Kalevi Holsti, *Peace and War: Armed Conflicts and International Order 1648-1989* (Cambridge, Eng.: Cambridge University Press, 1991), especially pp. 47-51, 85-89.

26. Bonney, *State Finance* and his (ed.), *The Rise of the Fiscal State in Europe, c.1200-1815* (Oxford: Oxford University Press, 1999), are the most comprehensive compilations of budgetary data. For war frequency, see Quincy Wright, *A Study of War* (Chicago: University of Chicago Press, 1942), p. 653.

27. Werner Sombart, *Krieg und Kapitalismus* (Munich: Duncker, 1913); John Nef, *War and Human Progress* (London: Routledge, 1950); and more briefly: John *Hale, War and Society in Renaissance Europe 1450-1620* (London: Fontana, 1985), chap. 8; Frank Tallett, *War and Society in Early-Modern Europe, 1495-1715* (London: Routledge, 1992), pp. 216-32.

28. My argument accords with that of Theda Skocpol, *States and Social Revolutions: A Comparative Analysis of France, Russia, and China* (Cambridge, Eng.: Cambridge University Press, 1979). Jack Goldstone, *Revolution and Rebellion in the Early Modern World* (Berkeley: University of California Press, 1991), misses the modernizing element of revolutions during modernity, as opposed to premodern times.

29. I am using the distinction coined by Mann in *The Sources of Social Power*.

30. Adam Ferguson, *An Essay on the History of Civil Society* (1767), especially parts v and vi.

31. Arguing that the East Asian civilizations did not fall behind Europe until industrialization, Pomeranz, *The Great Divergence*, does not pay sufficient attention to Francis Bacon's trio of modernity: gun powder, ocean navigation, and the printing press. Paul Bairoch, "European Gross National Product 1800-1975," *Journal of European Economic History*, 5 (1976): 287, roughly estimates that European per capita product was about 20 percent higher than Asia's in 1800. However, Maddison, *The World Economy*, pp. 28, 42, 44, 47, 49, 90, 126, 264, criticizes both Pomeranz and Bairoch, and calculates that Europe overtook Asia in per capita wealth around 1400, and

continuously widened its lead to twice the Asian per capita product by the eve of industrialization (thrice in the cases of the Netherlands and Britain).

32. For a beautiful overview, see Michael Howard, *War and the Liberal Conscience* (Oxford: Oxford University Press, 1981), chap. 1.

33. Jean Jacques Rousseau, "Abstract and Judgement of Saint Pierre's Project for Perpetual Peace" (1756), in S. Hoffmann and D. Fidler (eds.), *Rousseau on International Relations* (Oxford: Oxford University Press, 1991), pp. 53-100.

34. In Thomas Paine, *Rights of Man, Common Sense, and Other Political Writings* (Oxford: Oxford University Press, 1995), p. 212.

35. Ibid., pp. 195-96, 321.

36. Ibid., pp. 265-66; also see pp. 128-31, 227; Howard, *War and the Liberal Conscience*, p. 29; Thomas Walker, "The Forgotten Prophet: Tom Paine's Cosmopolitanism and International Relations," *International Studies Quarterly*, 44 (2000): 51-72.

37. In H. Reiss, ed., Kant's *Political Writings* (Cambridge, Eng.: Cambridge University Press, 1970), pp. 93-130.

3

1. These are my rough calculations based on the estimated data. The most comprehensive and update estimates are Angus Maddison, *The World Economy: A Millennial Perspective* (Paris: OECD, 2001), pp. 28, 90, 126, 183-86, 264-65. See also Paul Bairoch, "Europe's Gross National Product: 1800-1975," *Journal of European Economic History*, 5 (1976): 301; and Bairoch, "International Industrialization Levels from 1750 to 1980," ibid., 11 (1982), especially pp. 275, 284, 286; W. W. Rostow, *The World Economy: History & Prospect* (Austin: University of Texas, 1978), pp. 4-7, 48-49.

2. Melvin Small and David Singer, *Resort to Arms: International and Civil Wars, 1816-1980* (Beverly Hills, Calif.: SAGE, 1982), based on their important Correlates of War database, gives no basis for comparison to earlier times. On the other hand, addressing all the states in the global system during the past two centuries, it compares "apples and oranges" by encompassing the widest range of development—in effect different worlds. But see Jack Levy, *War in the Modern Great Power System, 1495-1975* (Lexington: University Press of Kentucky, 1983), especially pp. 112-49, which concentrates on the great powers' wars among themselves—the major wars by the most advanced states. Also Evan Luard, *War in International Society* (London: Tauris, 1986), pp. 53, 67.

3. For more detail see Azar Gat, *War in Human Civilization* (Oxford: Oxford University Press, 2006), pp. 524-29, 534-35.

4. Small and Singer, *Resort to Arms*, pp. 156-57, 198-201; Levy, *War in the Modern Great Power System*, pp. 136-37, 150-68; Luard, *War in International Society*, pp. 67-81.

5. John Stuart Mill, *Principles of Political Economy* (New York: Kelley, 1961), bk. II, chap. xvil, sect. 5, p. 582.

6. Auguste Comte, "Plan of the Scientific Operations Necessary for Reorganizing Society" (1822), and "Course de Philosophie Positive" (1832-42), in Gertrud Lenzer (ed.), *Auguste Comte and Positivism: The Essential Writings* (Chicago: University of Chicago Press, 1975), pp. 37, 293-97.

7. Cf. Kalevi Holsti, *Peace and War: Armed Conflict and International Order 1648-1989* (Cambridge, Eng.: Cambridge University Press, 1991), pp. 139-45.

8. Mary Townsend, *European Colonial Expansion since 1871* (Chicago: Lippincott, 1941), p. 19; D. K. Fieldhouse, *Economics and Empire 1830-1914* (Ithaca, N.Y.: Cornell University Press, 1973), p. 3; Daniel Headrick, *The Tools of Empire: Technology and European Imperialism in the Nineteenth Century* (New York: Oxford University Press, 1981), p. 3.

9. Headrick, *The Tools of Empire*.

10. Although sometimes historically crude, cf. Richard Rosecrance, *The Rise of the Trading State: Commerce and Conquest in the Modern World* (New York: Basic Books, 1986); also, Stephen Brooks, "The Globalization of Production and the Changing Benefits of Conquest," *Journal of Conflict Resolution*, 43.5 (Oct. 1999): 646-670.

11. Calculated on the basis of the data in B. R. Mitchell, *International Historical Statistics, Europe 1750-1988* (New York: Stockton, 1992), pp. 553-62; Maddison, *The World Economy*, pp. 126, 127, 184; Simon Kuznets, *Modern Economic Growth* (New Haven, Conn.: Yale University Press, 1966), pp. 306-307, 312-14.

12. John Gallagher and Ronald Robinson, "The Imperialism of Free Trade," *Economic History Review*, 4 (1953): 1-15.

13. Karl Marx and Friedrich Engels, "Manifesto of the Communist Party," in *Economic and Philosophical Manuscripts of 1844 and the Communist Manifesto* (Amherst, N.Y.: Prometheus, 1988), p. 213.

14. D. C. M. Platt, "The Imperialism of Free Trade: Some Reservations," *Economic History Review*, 21 (1968): 296-306; Platt, "Further Objections to an 'Imperialism of Free Trade,' 1830-60," ibid., 26 (1973): 77-91.

15. Gallagher and Robinson, "The Imperialism of Free Trade," p. 6.

16. Cf. Niall Ferguson, *Empire: The Rise and Demise of the British World Order and the Lessons for Global Power* (New York: Basic Books, 2002); Ferguson, *Colossus: The Price of American Empire* (New York: Penguin, 2004).

17. Ronald Robinson and John Gallagher, *Africa and the Victorians* (New York: St. Martin, 1961), p. 78.

18. Gallagher and Robinson, "The Imperialism of Free Trade," p. 13.

19. For a critique by the most confirmed free-trader among economic historians, see Patrick O'Brien, "The Costs and Benefits of British Imperialism, 1846-1914," *Past and Present*, 120 (1988): 163-200. Also, Paul Kennedy and Patrick O'Brien, "Debate: The Costs and Benefits of British Imperialism, 1846-1914," *Past and Present*, 125 (1989): 186-99.

20. Lance Davis and Robert Huttenback, *Mammon and the Pursuit of Empire: The Political Economy of British Imperialism, 1860-1912* (Cambridge, Eng.: Cambridge University Press, 1986), invalidate J. M. A. Hobson, *Imperialism: A Study* (Ann Arbor: University of Michigan Press, 1965 [1902]), and V. I. Lenin, *Imperialism: The Highest Stage of Capitalism* (New York: International Publishers, 1939). See also Fieldhouse, *Economics and Empire*. On France, Henri Brunschwig, *French Colonialism 1871-1914: Myths and Realities* (New York: Praeger, 1966), pp. 90-91, 96.

4

1. Two classical studies are: Hannah Arendt, *The Origins of Totalitarianism* (Cleveland, Oh.: Meridian, 1958); Carl Friedrich and Zbigniew Brzezinski, *Totalitarian Dictatorship and Autocracy* (Cambridge, Mass.: Harvard University Press, 1965).

2. *The Economist*, March 1, 2008, p. 25.

3. I am using the categories suggested by William Baumal, Robert Litman, and Carl Schramm, *Good Capitalism, Bad Capitalism and the Economy of Growth and Prosperity* (New Haven, Conn.: Yale University Press, 2007), especially chap. 4.

4. Alan Greenspan, *The Age of Turbulence* (New York: Penguin, 2007), p. 275.

5. Michael Mandelbaum, *Democracy's Good Name: The Rise and Risks of the World's Most Popular Form of Government* (New York: Public Affairs, 2007), pp. 114-118.

6. Ibid., pp. 96-100; Francis Fukuyama, *The End of History and the Last Man* (New York: Free Press, 1992), chap. 27; Robert Dahl, *On Democracy* (New Haven, Conn.: Yale University Press, 1998), pp. 173-79.

7. Ronald Inglehart and Christian Welzel, "How Development Leads to Democracy," *Foreign Affairs*, March-April 2009, based on their important comprehensive surveys of world values and recent book: *Modernization, Cultural Change, and Democracy: The Human Development Sequence* (Cambridge, Eng.: Cambridge University Press, 2005).

8. Merle Goldman, *From Comrade to Citizen: The Struggle for Political Rights in China* (Cambridge, Mass., Harvard University Press, 2005); John Thornton, "Long Time Coming: The Prospects for Democracy in China," *Foreign Affairs*, Jan.-Feb. 2008; James Mann, *The China Fantasy: Why Capitalism Will Not Bring Democracy to China* (New York: Penguin, 2008), many arguments in which are similar to mine. A broad survey of relevant aspects can be found in Cheng Li (ed.), *China's Changing Political Landscape: Prospects for Democracy* (Washington: Brookings, 2008).

9. J. Damm and S. Thomas, (eds.), *Chinese Cyberspaces: Technological Changes and Political Effects* (New York: Routledge, 2006); Johan Lagerkvist, "Internet Ideotainment in PRC: National Responses to Cultural Globalization," *Journal of Contemporary China*, 17 (2008): 121-140.

10. Fareed Zakaria, *The Post American World* (New York: Norton, 2008), p. 83.

11. See, for example, Susan Shirk, *China: Fragile Superpower* (New York: Oxford University Press, 2007).

12. *The Economist*, Aug. 2, 2008, p. 27.

13. Adam Przeworski, Michael Alvarez, Jose Cheibub, and Fernando Limongi, *Democracy and Development* (Cambridge, Eng.: Cambridge University Press, 2000).

14. John Ikenberry, "The Rise of China and the Future of the West: Can the Liberal System Survive?" *Foreign Affairs*, Jan.-Feb. 2008.

15. Guillermo O'Donnell, *Modernization and Bureaucratic-Authoritarianism: Studies in South American Politics* (Berkeley: University of California Press, 1973).

16. Robert Taylor (ed.), *The Idea of Freedom in Asia and Africa* (Stanford: Stanford University Press, 2002).

17. Joshua Kurlantzick, *Charm Offensive: How China's Soft Power Is Transforming the World* (New Haven, Conn.: Yale University Press, 2007).

18. In the meantime, this has been developed by both Zakaria, *The Post American World*, and Walter Russell Mead, *God and Gold: Britain, America, and the Making of the Modern World* (New York: Knopf, 2007), chap. 20.

19. The relationship between GDP, GDP per capita, and national power, is developed in Azar Gat, *War in Human Civilization* (Oxford: Oxford University Press, 2006), pp. 515-24.

5

1. For the major initial statements of the thesis see: Dean Babst, "A Force for Peace," *Industrial Research*, 14 (April 1972): 55-58; Melvin Small and David Singer, "The War-Proneness of Democratic Regimes, 1816-1965," *Jerusalem Journal of International Relations*, 1.4 (1976): 50-69; R. J. Rummel, "Libertarianism and International Violence," *Journal of Conflict Resolution*, 27 (1983): 27-71; Michael Doyle, "Kant, Liberal Legacies, and Foreign Affairs," *Philosophy and Public Affairs*, 12 (1983): 205-35, 323-53; Steve Chan, "Mirror, Mirror on the Wall: Are the Free Countries More Pacific?" *Journal of Conflict Resolution*, 28 (1984): 617-48; William Domke, *War and the Changing Global System* (New Haven, Conn.: Yale University Press, 1988); Zeev Maoz and Nasrin Abdolali, "Regime Type and International Conflict 1816-1976," *Journal of Conflict Resolution*, 33 (1989): 3-35; Zeev Maoz and Bruce Russett, "Normative and Structural Causes of Democratic Peace 1946-1986," *American Political Science Review*, 87 (1993): 624-38; Bruce Russett, *Grasping the Democratic Peace* (Princeton, N.J.: Princeton University Press, 1993). For the expansion of the initial thesis to militarized disputes in general see: Gregory Raymond, "Democracies, Disputes, and Third-Party Intermediaries," *Journal of Conflict Resolution*, 38 (1994): 24-42; William Dixon, "Democracy and the Peaceful Settlement of International Conflict," *American Political Science Review*, 88 (1994): 14-32; David Rousseau, Christopher Gelpi, Dan Reiter, and Paul Huth, "Assessing the Dyadic Nature of the Democratic Peace, 1918-1988," *American Political Science Review*, 90 (1996): 512-33; Jean-Sebastien Rioux, "A Crisis-Based Evaluation of the Democratic Peace Proposition," *Canadian Journal of Political Science*, 31 (1998): 263-83; Michael Mousseau, "Democracy and Compromise in Militarized Interstate Conflicts, 1816-1992," *Journal of Conflict Resolution*, 42 (1998): 210-30.

2. For the critics see: Christopher Layne, "Kant or Cant: The Myth of the Democratic Peace," *International Security*, 19.2 (1994): 5-49; Layne, "Lord Palmerston and the Triumph of Realism: Anglo-French Relations, 1830-48," in M. Elman (ed.), *Paths to Peace: Is Democracy the Answer?* (Cambridge, Mass.: MIT Press, 1997), pp. 61-100; David Spiro, "The Insignificance of the Liberal Peace," *International Security*, 19.2 (1994): 50-86; Raymond Cohen, "Pacific Unions: A Reappraisal of the Theory that 'Democracies Do Not Go to War with Each Other,'" *Review of International Studies*, 20 (1994): 207-23; Ido Oren, "From Democracy to Demon: Changing American Perceptions of Germany during World War I," *International Security*, 20.2 (1995): 147-84; Henry Faber and Joanne Gowa, "Politics and Peace," ibid., 20.2 (1995): 123-46; Joanne Gowa, *Battles and Bullets: The Elusive Democratic Peace* (Princeton, N.J.: Princeton University Press, 1999). For the democratic peace theorists' response, see: Russet, *Grasping the Democratic Peace*, pp. 16-19; John Owen, "How Liberalism Produces Democratic Peace," *International Security*, 19.2 (1994): 87-125, Owen, *Liberal Peace, Liberal War* (Ithaca, N.Y.: Cornell University Press, 1997); James Ray, *Democracy and International Conflict: An Evaluation of the Democratic Peace Proposition* (Columbia: University of South Carolina Press, 1995); Zeev Maoz, "The Controversy over the Democratic Peace: Rearguard Action or Cracks in the Wall?" *International Security*, 22.1 (1997): 162-98; Bruce Russett and John Oneal, *Triangulating Peace: Democracy, Interdependence and International Organizations* (New York: Norton, 2001), pp. 111-14.

3. Edward Mansfield and Jack Snyder, "Democratization and the Danger of War," *International Security*, 20.1 (1995): 5-38; Jack Snyder, *From Voting to Violence: Democratization and Nationalist Conflict* (New York: Norton, 2000); Edward Mansfield and Jack Snyder, *Electing to Fight: Why Emerging Democracies Go to War* (Cambridge, Mass: MIT Press, 2005), (while that book is intended to correct their much-criticized earlier statistics, it still curiously fails to grasp that national self-determination is a natural aspiration of free peoples, regarding it instead as pure elite manipulation); Kurt Gaubatz, *Elections and War: The Electoral Incentives in the Democratic Politics of War and Peace* (Stanford, Calif.: Stanford University Press, 1999), chap. 2; Paul Huth and Todd Allee, *The Democratic Peace and Territorial Conflict in the Twentieth Century* (New York: Cambridge University Press, 2002). Others have contended that it was regime change in general rather than the democratic transition that accounts for greater belligerency, or dispute the evidence on various grounds: Zeev Maoz, "Joining the Club of Nations: Political Development and International Conflict, 1816-1976," *International Studies Quarterly*, 33 (1989): 199-231; Stephen Walt, *Revolution and War* (Ithaca, N.Y.: Cornell University Press, 1996); Andrew Enterline, "Driving while Democratizing," *International Security*, 20.4 (1996): 183-96; Enterline, "Regime Changes and Interstate Conflict, 1816-1992," *Political Research Quarterly*, 51 (1998): 385-409; Enterline and Michael Greig, "Beacons of Hope? The Impact of Imposed Democracy on Regional Peace, Democracy, and Prosperity," *Journal of Politics*, 67

(2005): 1075-98; Kristian Gleditsch and Michael Ward, "War and Peace in Space and Time: The Role of Democratization," *International Studies Quarterly*, 44 (2000): 1-29; Michael Ward and Kristian Gleditsch, "Democratizing for Peace," *American Political Science Review*, 92 (1988): 51-61; Russett and Oneal, *Triangulating Peace*, pp. 51-52, 116-22; John Oneal, Bruce Russett, and Michael Berbaum, "Causes of Peace: Democracy, Interdependence, and International Organizations, 1885-1992," *International Studies Quarterly*, 47 (2003): 371-93, especially 383-84; Sara Mitchell and Brandon Prins, "Beyond Territorial Contiguity: Issues at Stake in Democratic Militarized Interstate Disputes," *International Studies Quarterly*, 43 (1999): 169-83; David Rousseau, *Democracy and War* (Stanford, Calif.: Stanford University Press, 2005), chap. 6.

4. Maoz and Abdolali, "Regime Type and International Conflict"; Steve Chan, "In Search of Democratic Peace: Problems and Promise," *Mershon International Studies Review*, 41 (1997): 83.

5. For the correlation between the level of liberalism and peace, see Rummel, "Libertarianism and International Violence"; Rummel, *Power Kills: Democracy as a Method of Nonviolence* (New Brunswick, N.J.: Transaction, 1997), p. 5 and chap. 3. For historical gradualism, see Bruce Russet and Zeev Maoz, incorporated in Russet, *Grasping the Democratic Peace*, pp. 72-73; more fully developed in Maoz, "The Controversy over the Democratic Peace"; and integral in Russett and Oneal, *Triangulating Peace*, pp. 111-14.

6. Russet and Maoz, in Russet, *Grasping the Democratic Peace*, p. 86. Generally regarding today's developing world: Edward Friedman, "The Painful Gradualness of Democratization: Proceduralism as a Necessary Discontinuous Revolution," in H. Handelman and M. Tessler (eds.), *Democracy and Its Limits: Lessons from Asia, Latin America, and the Middle East* (Notre Dame, Indiana: University of Notre Dame Press, 1999), pp. 321-40.

7. On the pros and cons: see Kenneth Waltz, *Theory of International Politics* (Reading, Mass.: Addison, 1979), pp. 212-15; Doyle, "Kant, Liberal Legacies, and Foreign Affairs," pp. 231-32; Edward Mansfield, *Power, Trade, and War* (Princeton, N.J.: Princeton University Press, 1994); Katherine Barbieri, "Economic Interdependence: A Path to Peace or a Source of Interstate Conflict?" *Journal of Peace Research*, 33 (1996): 29-49; Dale Copeland, "Economic Interdependence and War: A Theory of Trade Expectations," *International Security*, 20.4 (1996): 5-41; Edward Mansfield and Brian Pollins (eds.), *Economic Interdependence and International Conflict* (Ann Arbor: University of Michigan Press, 2003); Solomon Polachek, "Why Democracies Cooperate More and Fight Less: The Relationship between Trade and International Cooperation," *Review of International Economics*, 5 (1997): 295-309; Katherine Barbieri and Gerald Schneider, "Globalization and Peace: Assessing New Directions in the Study of Trade and Conflict," *Journal of Peace Research*, 36

(1999): 387-404; Erik Gartzke, "The Capitalist Peace," *American Journal of Political Science*, 51 (Jan. 2007): 166-91.

8. This was originally demonstrated by Domke, *War and the Changing Global System*, and impressively elaborated by Russett and Oneal, *Triangulating Peace*.

9. The best studies are: Michael Mousseau, "Market Prosperity, Democratic Consolidation, and Democratic Peace," *Journal of Conflict Resolution*, 44 (2000): 472-507; Mousseau, "The Nexus of Market Society, Liberal Preferences, and Democratic Peace," *International Studies Quarterly*, 47 (2003): 483-510; Mousseau, "Comparing New Theory with Prior Beliefs: Market Civilization and the Democratic Peace," *Conflict Management and Peace Science*, 22 (2005): 63-77; Mousseau, Håvard Hegre, and John Oneal, "How the Wealth of Nations Conditions the Liberal Peace," *European Journal of International Relations*, 9 (2003): 277-314; Gartzke, "The Capitalist Peace." See also Polachek, "Why Democracies Cooperate More and Fight Less"; Håvard Hegre, "Development and the Liberal Peace: What Does It Take to Be a Trading State?" *Journal of Peace Research*, 37 (2000): 5-30. Kenneth Benoit, "Democracies Really are More Pacific (in General)," *Journal of Conflict Resolution*, 40 (1996): 636-57, is limited to the years 1960-1980.

10. Errol Henderson and David Singer, "Civil War in the Post-Colonial World, 1946-92," *Journal of Peace Research*, 37 (2000): 275-99; Errol Henderson, *Democracy and War: The End of an Illusion* (Boulder, Colo.: Lynne Rienner, 2002), chap. 5.

11. Mousseau, "Market Prosperity"; Gary Marks and Larry Diamond (eds.), *Reexamining Democracy* (Newbury Park, Calif.: Sage, 1992).

12. Adam Przeworski, Michael Alvarez, Jose Cheibub, and Fernando Limongi, *Democracy and Development* (Cambridge, Eng.: Cambridge University Press, 2000), point out that democracy exists in all levels of development; yet this is true on a country scale only within the framework of modernizing development, never before.

13. Fareed Zakaria, "The Rise of Illiberal Democracy," *Foreign Affairs*, 76.6 (1997): 22-46; Zakaria, *The Future of Freedom: Illiberal Democracy at Home and Abroad* (New York: Norton, 2004); Larry Diamond, *Developing Democracy* (Baltimore, Md.: Johns Hopkins University Press, 1999), especially pp. 34-60, 279-80.

14. Bruce Russett and William Antholis, "The Imperfect Democratic Peace of Ancient Greece," reprinted in Russett, *Grasping the Democratic Peace*, chap. 3.

15. Spencer Weart, *Never at War: Why Democracies Will not Fight One Another* (New Haven, Conn.: Yale University Press, 1998). This highly problematic

work was criticized by Eric Robinson, a leading expert on early Greek democracies: "Reading and Misreading the Ancient Evidence for Democratic Peace," *Journal of Peace Research*, 38 (2001): 593-608. A short exchange resulted: Weart, ibid., pp. 609-13; Robinson, ibid., pp. 615-17. See also the criticism by the leading authority on the Greek polis and fourth century BC Athenian democracy: Mogens Hansen and Thomas Nielsen, *An Inventory of Archaic and Classical Poleis* (Oxford: Oxford University Press, 2004), pp. 84-85.

16. Weart, *Never at War*, p. 246, postpones any mention of the first Athenian Empire to as late in his book as possible, and then summarily disposes of this inconvenience. The problem was better acknowledged by: Russett and Antholis; Tobias Bachteler, "Explaining the Democratic Peace: The Evidence from Ancient Greece Reviewed," *Journal of Peace Research*, 34 (1997): 315-23; and is addressed in Lorem Samons, *What's Wrong with Democracy? From Athenian Practice to American Worship* (Berkeley: University of California Press, 2004).

17. Alexander Yakobson, *Elections and Electioneering in Rome* (Stuttgart, Germany: Steiner, 1999).

18. Weart, *Never at War*, mentions Rome only once in his appendix of problematic cases (p. 297), where he lamely excuses himself from discussing it on the grounds that we lack information about Carthage.

19. Doyle, "Kant, Liberal Legacies, and Foreign Affairs," p. 212.

20. David Sobek, "Regime Type, Preferences, and War: An Empirical Analysis of Renaissance Italy," *Journal of Conflict Resolution*, 47.2 (2003): 204-225; this is far more reliable than Weart.

21. Russett and Oneal, *Triangulating Peace*, chap. 1.

22. See chap. 3 of this book, p.40.

23. Peter Liberman, *Does Conquest Pay? The Exploitation of Occupied Industrial Societies* (Princeton, N.J.: Princeton University Press, 1996). Stephen Brooks's criticism in "The Globalization of Production and the Changing Benefits of Conquest," *Journal of Conflict Resolution*, 43.5 (Oct. 1999): 646-670, is only partly persuasive. The Soviet Union's empire may or may not have been economically beneficial for the country, but Brooks fails to note that this was predominantly because the empire was communist; that is, the empire, like the Soviet Union itself, was economically dysfunctional. Nor is he convincing in claiming that the wealth of countries that constitute only part of a global production chain is difficult to retain under alien rule. Consider, for example, the change of hands in Hong Kong.

24. Both Small and Singer, "The War-Proneness of Democratic Regimes," and Chan, "Mirror, Mirror on the Wall," noted that difference, while pointing out that democracies initiated wars nearly as often as non-democracies. But R. J. Rummel's counter-claim in "Libertarianism and Interstate Violence" and *Power Kills*—that liberal countries are more peaceful in general—is corroborated by Domke, *War and the Changing Global System*; Stuart Bremer, "Dangerous Dyads: Conditions Affecting the Likelihood of Interstate War, 1816-1965," *Journal of Conflict Resolution*, 36 (1992): 309-41; Benoit, "Democracies Really Are More Pacific"; Rousseau et al., "Assessing the Dyadic Nature of the Democratic Peace"; Rousseau, *Democracy and War*; Rioux, "A Crisis-Based Evaluation of the Democratic Peace Proposition"; Russett, altering his initial position, in Russett and Oneal, *Triangulating Peace*, pp. 49-50.

25. Noted by Small and Singer, "The War-Proneness of Democratic Regimes," pp. 63-64; and developed by Rummel, *Power Kills*.

26. Rousseau, *Democracy and War*.

27. Rummel, *Power Kills*; Mathew Krain and Marrissa Myers, "Democracy and Civil War: A Note on the Democratic Peace Proposition," *International Interaction*, 23 (1997): 109-18, failing to distinguish between advanced and less advanced democracies; well noted in Tanja Ellingson, "Colorful Community or Ethnic Witches-Brew? Multiethnicity and Domestic Conflict during and after the Cold War," *Journal of Conflict Resolution*, 44 (2000): 228-49; Ted Gurr, *Minorities at Risk: A Global View of Ethnopolitical Conflicts* (Washington: U.S. Institute of Peace, 1993); Errol Henderson and David Singer, "Civil War in the Post-Colonial World"; Henderson, *Democracy and War*, chap. 5.

28. Rummel, *Power Kills*.

29. B. R. Mitchell, *European Historical Statistics* 1750-1970 (London: Macmillan, 1975), pp. B6 and B7.

30. For the statistics, see Friedrich von Bernhardi, *Germany and the Next War* (New York: Longmans, 1914), pp. 243-44.

31. Bill Bishop, "Who Goes to War," *Washington Post*, November 16, 2003; Ann Scott Tyson, "Youths in Rural U.S. Are Drawn to Military," ibid., November 10, 2005. The second article emphasizes the recruits' poor economic background but not their rural roots.

32. Richard Rosecrance, *The Rise of the Virtual State* (New York: Basic Books, 1999), p. xii; also p. 26 for the other major industrial countries; Robert Gilpin, *The Challenge of Global Capitalism* (Princeton, N.J.: Princeton University Press, 2000), p. 33.

33. For the Soviets, see Anthony Beevor, *The Fall of Berlin* 1945 (New York: Penguin, 2003), p. 410. For the Americans and Japanese in World War II, see Joshua Goldstein, *War and Gender: How Gender Shapes the War System and Vice Versa* (New York: Cambridge University Press), pp. 337, 346, respectively.

34. Herbert Moller, "Youth as a Force in the Modern World," *Comparative Studies in Society and History*, 10 (1967/8): 237-60; Christian Mesquida and Neil Wiener, "Human Collective Aggression: A Behavioral Ecology Perspective," *Ethology and Sociobiology*, 17 (1996): 247-62.

35. Mitchell, *European Historical Statistics*, section B2, especially pp. 37 and 52; United Nations, *World Population Prospects: The 2000 Revision* (New York: UN, 2001).

36. Samuel Huntington, *The Clash of Civilizations and the Remaking of World Order* (New York: Simon and Schuster, 1997), pp. 116-20.

37. Edward Luttwak, "Blood and Computers: The Crisis of Classical Military Power in Advanced Postindustrialist Societies," in Zeev Maoz and Azar Gat (eds.), *War in a Changing World* (Ann Arbor, University of Michigan Press, 2001), pp. 49-75.

38. Lisa Brandes, "Public Opinion, International Security and Gender: The United States and Great Britain since 1945," unpublished doctoral dissertation, Yale University, 1994.

39. Bruce Russet, "The Democratic Peace—And Yet It Moves," in M. Brown, S. Lynn-Jones, and S. Miller (eds.), *Debating the Democratic Peace* (Cambridge, Mass.: MIT Press, 1996), p. 340; Doyle, "Michael Doyle on the Democratic Peace—Again," ibid., p. 372.

40. Mark Tessler and Ira Warriner, "Gender, Feminism, and Attitudes towards International Conflict," *World Politics*, 49 (1997): 250-81; Mark Tessler, Jodi Nachtwey, and Audra Grant, "Further Tests of the Women and Peace Hypothesis: Evidence from Cross-National Survey Research in the Middle East," *International Studies Quarterly*, 43 (1999): 519-31.

41. Thomas Knock, *To End All Wars: Woodrow Wilson and the Quest for a New World Order* (New York: Oxford University Press, 1992), pp. 26-28; and generally, Tony Smith, *America's Mission: The United States and the Worldwide Struggle for Democracy in the Twentieth Century* (Princeton, N.J.: Princeton University Press, 1994), chap. 3.

42. Cf. Francis Fukuyama, *State Building: Governance and World Order in the 21st Century* (Ithaca, N.Y.: Cornell University Press, 2004), pp. 38-39, 92-93.

6

1. Randall Schweller, "Domestic Structure and Preventive War: Are Democracies More Pacific?" *World Politics*, 44 (1992): 235-69.

2. David Hume, "Of the Balance of Power," in his *Essays: Literary, Moral and Political* (London: Routledge, 1894), pp. 202-203; Michael Doyle, *Ways of War and Peace: Realism, Liberalism, and Socialism* (New York: Norton, 1997), pp. 275-77.

3. John Gaddis, "The Origins of Self-Deterrence: The United States and the Non-Use of Nuclear Weapons, 1945-1958," in his *The Long Peace: Inquiries Into the History of the Cold War* (New York: Oxford University Press, 1987), pp. 104-146.

4. John Mueller, *Retreat from Doomsday: The Obsolescence of Major War* (New York: Basic Books, 1989).

5. *Contra* Mueller, *Retreat from Doomsday*, pp. 53-68.

6. All this is insufficiently addressed in Richard Rosecrance (ed.), *The New Great Power Coalition: Toward a World Concert of Nations* (Lanham, Md.: Rowman, 2001).

7. David French, *British Strategy and War Aims, 1914-1916* (London: Allen and Unwin, 1986).

8. This is the subject of part II of Azar Gat, *Fascist and Liberal Visions of War* (Oxford: Oxford University Press, 1998); incorporated in Gat, *A History of Military Thought* (Oxford: Oxford University Press, 2001).

9. David Reynolds, *The Creation of the Anglo-American Alliance, 1937-1941* (London: Europa, 1981), especially pp. 17, 30-31, 35; Robert Dallek, *Franklin D. Roosevelt and American Foreign Policy, 1932-1945* (New York: Oxford University Press, 1979), especially pp. 163-64; Callum Macdonald, "Deterrence Diplomacy: Roosevelt and the Containment of Germany, 1938-1940," in R. Boyce and E. Robertson (eds.), *Paths to War: New Essays on the Origins of the Second World War* (London: Macmillan, 1989), pp. 297-329; D. C. Watt, *Succeeding John Bull: America in Britain's Place, 1900-1975* (Cambridge, Eng.: Cambridge University Press, 1984), pp. 82-83.

10. George Kennan, *American Diplomacy* (Chicago: University of Chicago Press, 1985 [1951]), pp. vi-vii.

7

1. The thesis developed here was originally put forward by Gil Merom, *How Democracies Lose Small Wars: State, Society, and the Failure of France in Algeria, Israel in Lebanon, and the United States in Vietnam* (New York: Cambridge University Press, 2003). While presenting a well-crafted argument about strategic interaction, Ivan Arreguin-Toft, *How the Weak Win Wars: A Theory of Asymmetrical Conflict* (New York: Cambridge University Press, 2005), in effect ends up corroborating Merom's thesis. What he terms a strategy of "barbarism" turns out in his analysis to be the chief method of suppressing counterinsurgency. Indeed, his statistics indicate a sharp decline in successful counterinsurgency since the nineteenth century, correlating with the decline in the application of barbarism, particularly, as he admits, by democracies. See especially pp. xi-xii, 4, 33, 37, 204, 225.

2. David Edelstein, *Occupational Hazards: Success and Failure in Military Occupation* (Ithaca, N.Y.: Cornell University Press, 2008), is a recent example of the common blind spot for the role of democracy. As it apparently does not occur to him that the cause may lie precisely in this factor, all his case studies except for one involve a modern democratic occupier, which usually fails unless the occupier and occupied share enough common interests or common enemies. The only case study that involves a nondemocratic country, and could serve as a control, is that of the Soviet Union in North Korea in the immediate aftermath of World War II (and longer in Eastern Europe). The author concludes that in contrast to the U.S.'s failure in South Korea during that same time, the Soviet occupier succeeded—indeed, easily and cheaply—because of its effective suppression capability.

3. Thucydides, iii. 37.

4. Harold Selesky, "Colonial America," in M. Howard, G. Andreopoulos, and M. Shulman (eds.), *The Laws of War: Constraints on Warfare in the Western World* (New Haven, Conn.: Yale University Press, 1994), chap. 5.

5. Merom, *How Democracies Lose Small Wars*, p. 61.

6. Richard Shannon, *Gladstone and the Bulgarian Agitation 1876* (Hassocks, Eng.: Harvester, 1975).

7. James Ray and Ayse Vural, "Power Disparities and Paradoxical Conflict Outcomes," *International Interactions*, 12 (1986): 315-42.

8. Glenn Snyder, "Crisis Bargaining," in C. Hermann (ed.), *International Crises: Insights from Behavioral Research* (New York: Free Press, 1972), p. 232; Steven Rosen, "War Power and the Willingness to Suffer," in B. Russett (ed.), *Peace, War, and Numbers* (Beverly Hills, Calif.: Sage, 1972), pp. 167-83; Andrew

Mack, "Why Big Nations Lose Small Wars: The Politics of Asymmetrical Conflict," *World Politics*, 27 (1975): 175-200.

9. For revisionist reappraisals of the alleged critical role of television in Vietnam see: Daniel C. Hallin, *The "Uncensored War": The Media and Vietnam* (Berkeley: University of California Press, 1986); William Hammond, *Reporting Vietnam: Media and Military at War* (Lawrence: University of Kansas, 1998).

10. Dan Reiter and Allan Stam, *Democracies at War* (Princeton, N.J.: Princeton University Press, 2002), chap. 7.

11. Alexander Downes, *Targeting Civilians in War* (Ithaca, N.Y.: Cornell University Press, 2008), is thoroughly supported by statistics. Yet the author does not allow the clear change in the trend during the second half of the twentieth century, which he documents, to alter his general pronouncement regarding the somewhat greater propensity of democracies to target civilians. In a book concentrating on interstate wars, he devotes one chapter to counterinsurgency warfare, and in it repeats his argument that democracies are no different with respect to the targeting of civilians. Yet not only is his sole, early case study the Boer War in South Africa; he also fails to consider that just a few years later, Germany crushed insurgencies in both Namibia and Tanzania through genocidal means. Indeed, although acknowledging that nondemocracies alone are prone to mass killings in the millions, Downes does not weigh numbers in his statistical analysis. He takes no account of the actual percentages killed and, moreover, of the guerrilla wars deterred or cut short by nondemocracies' threat of mass killings. For the strong selection bias created by such omissions, see pp.144-45 below.

12. J. Moor and H. Wesseling (eds.), *Imperialism and War: Essays in Colonial Wars in Asia and Africa* (Leiden, Netherlands: Brill, 1989), pp. 87-120 (especially p. 106 for suppression techniques and atrocities), 121-45 (especially p. 141), 146-67 (especially p. 157).

13. Jon Bridgman, *The Revolt of the Hereros* (Berkeley: University of California, 1981); Horst Drechsler, *"Let Us Die Fighting": The Struggle of the Herero and Nama against German Imperialism, 1884-1915* (London: Zed, 1980); John Iliffe, *Tanganyika under German Rule 1905-1912* (Cambridge, Eng.: Cambridge University Press, 1969), pp. 9-29; and G. Gwassa and J. Iliffe (eds.), *Record of the Maji Maji Rising* (Nairobi: East African Publishing House, 1967).

14. Geoffrey Best, *Humanity in Warfare* (London: Methuen, 1983), pp. 226-28, 235-37, and chaps. III-IV in general.

15. Peter Liberman, *Does Conquest Pay? The Exploitation of Occupied Industrial Societies* (Princeton, N.J.: Princeton University Press, 1996).

16. H. Jack (ed.), *The Gandhi Reader* (Bloomington: Indiana University Press, 1956), pp. 317-22, 332-39, 344-47.

17. Michael Walzer, *Just and Unjust War* (New York: Basic Books, 1977) chap. 11, intelligently discusses the moral dilemmas involved, which in effect apply only to liberal societies.

9

1. See, for example, Walter Laqueur's otherwise excellent, *The New Terrorism: Fanaticism and the Arms of Mass Destruction* (New York: Oxford University Press, 1999), pp. 8-12.

2. Philip Cohen, "A Terrifying Power," *New Scientist*, Jan. 30, 1999, p. 10; Rachel Nowak, "Disaster in the Making," ibid., Jan. 13, 2001, pp. 4-5; Carina Dennis, "The Bugs of War," *Nature*, May 17, 2001, pp. 232-35.

3. Michael Moodie, "The Chemical Weapons Threat," in S. Drell, A. Sofaer, and G. Wilson (eds.), *The New Terror: Facing the Threat of Biological and Chemical Weapons* (Stanford, Calif.: Hoover Institution Press, 1999), p. 19.

4. Nadine Gurr and Benjamin Cole, *The New Face of Terrorism: Threats from Weapons of Mass Destruction* (London: Tauris, 2000), p. 43.

5. Anonymous scientist cited by Anne Applebaum, "The Next Plague," *The Washington Post*, Feb. 18, 2004.

6. Spencer Hsu, "Modest Gains against Ever-Present Bioterrorism Threat," *The Washington Post*, Aug. 3, 2008.

7. David Kaplan, "Aum Shinrikyo," in J. Tucker (ed.), *Toxic Terror: Assessing Terrorist Use of Chemical and Biological Weapons* (Cambridge, Mass.: MIT Press, 2000), chap. 12; Gurr and Cole, *New Face of Terrorism*, p. 51.

8. David Ignatius, "Portents of a Nuclear Al-Qaeda," *The Washington Post*, Oct. 18, 2007, p. A25.

9. Graham Allison, *Nuclear Terrorism: The Ultimate Preventable Catastrophe* (New York: Times Books, 2004), is a proposed blueprint for such a strategy. More generally: Philip Bobbitt, *The Shield of Achilles: War, Peace, and the Course of History* (London: Allen Lane, 2002); Bobbitt, *Terror and Consent: The Wars for the Twenty-First Century* (New York: Knopf, 2008).

10. See, for example, Scott D. Sagan (against) and Kenneth N. Waltz (for), *The Spread of Nuclear Weapons* (New York: Norton, 1999); references to terrorist nuclear threat have been added in the second edition (2003), pp. 126-30, 159-66. Also, (for) Martin van Creveld, *Nuclear Proliferation and the Future of Conflict* (New York: Free Press, 1993); and a good, balanced treatment by Devin Hagertly, *The Consequences of Nuclear Proliferation* (Cambridge, Mass., MIT Press, 1998).

11. Much of this is portrayed in Robert Kagan, *Of Paradise and Power: America and Europe in the New World Order* (London: Atlantic, 2003).

12. The case for the U.S. is best made by Michael Mandelbaum, *The Case for Goliath: How America Acts as the World's Government in the Twenty-First Century* (New York: Public Affairs, 2005).

13. *The Independent*, March 16, 2009.

14. Hsu, "Modest Gains."

10

1. Azar Gat, *War in Human Civilization* (Oxford: Oxford University Press, 2006), pp. 515-24.

2. David Lake, "Powerful Pacifists: Democratic States and War," *American Political Science Review*, 86 (1992): 24-37. I disagree with almost everything else in the article.

3. See note 1.

Index